MODEL RAILWAY OPERATION

As part of our ongoing market research, we are always pleased to receive comments about our books, suggestions for new titles, or requests for catalogues. Please write to: The Editorial Director, Patrick Stephens Limited, Sparkford, Near Yeovil, Somerset BA22 7JJ.

MODEL RAILWAY

OPERATION

IN ACCORDANCE WITH PROTOTYPE PRACTICE

C. J. FREEZER

Patrick Stephens Limited

First published in 1993
Reprinted 1995, 2000

British Library Cataloguing-in-Publication Data:
A catalogue record for this book is
available from the British Library.

ISBN 1 85260 421 1

Patrick Stephens Limited is an imprint of Haynes Publishing,
Sparkford, Nr Yeovil, Somerset BA22 7JJ.

Typeset by G&M, Raunds, Northamptonshire
Printed in Great Britain by
Butler & Tanner Limited, Frome and London

Contents

Introduction

Railway modelling differs from all other transport modelling fields in one vital respect; it is a practical proposition to simulate the operation of the prototype. Agreed, many ship and aircraft modellers do produce working models and frequently mimic some aspects of full-size operation, but the simulation is limited to the more obvious and elementary features. About the only area where a reasonable simulation is carried out as a matter of routine is with radio-controlled racing cars, but even here the differences between a model and full-size grand prix race are obvious to the lay observer.

Not only is it possible to operate a model railway exactly in accordance with full-size practice with only one significant difference (we have yet to devise a satisfactory means of entraining and detraining passengers), but also most of this can be done by one individual using nothing more elaborate than standard ready-to-run equipment available in any high street in the country. When a layout is operated by a trained team in accordance with a prototype-based operating schedule, the end product to the observer is an accurate simulation of the real thing. Indeed, to many serious operators, it *is* the real thing.

It is necessary to emphasize that this book is written in England by an Englishman, and inevitably the bias is

Operation in progress. Peter Denny at the controls of 'Buckingham'.

Period operation. LNWR 'Prince of Wales' 4-6-0, at the head of a London-bound express formed of Wolverton-built coaches in the LNWR's attractive two-colour livery, rolls majestically through this 4 mm scale model of Berkhamstead station.

towards British prototype practice. However, in operation the differences in national practice are less marked than they are in any other field, for the simple reason that railway operation is basic; the methods are those imposed by the nature of a railway. There are superficial differences, many created by national safety-oriented legislation, but the fundamentals are of universal application. If anyone questions this, consider that the waybill system of freight train operation was devised in the USA to accord with their prototype operating practices, and has been translated, without any significant modification, to British practice.

It is also necessary to point out that this book deals with the operation of a model, not a full-size system. Just as in the absence of working model passengers and horses, there are some aspects of the prototype that we quietly skate around, so there are operating procedures that are simple on the model but totally impracticable in real life — the concept of the fiddle yard

being the most obvious example. Even more to the point, we must never forget that the most under-resourced full-size operator has far better facilities at its disposal than most model railways, where limitations of space and finance set the bounds.

I have included a number of layout plans to illustrate methods of operation. They are less detailed than those I usually provide so that attention is drawn to the essential railway buildings and rail-connected industry. The majority are steam age concepts. This is because modern British operation is greatly simplified, and there is less emphasis on shunting and train reformation. With one exception, the plans assume 4 mm scale, and in most cases the radii employed make OO gauge the preferable option. A 300 mm (12 in) grid is superimposed to provide an indication of size. I am aware these dimensions are not identical, but the difference to a project plan reproduced to a very small scale is in practice immaterial.

Readers will realize that my prototype references are confined to the south and west of England. The reason is simple; these are the areas best known to me, but similar arrangements took place elsewhere because railway operation in Britain was fairly standardized.

Finally, I wish to thank my eldest son Nicholas for invaluable professional advice throughout the preparation of this book, and in particular for his painstaking checking of the final manuscript and for the improvements he has suggested as a result.

Cyril Freezer
Hemel Hempstead 1993

CHAPTER 1

On playing trains

Some 50 years ago it was usual to see short features in the popular press around Easter time headed 'Grown men play trains'. This was the normal way of heading a write-up of the Model Railway Exhibition, forerunner of today's IMREX, which thankfully gets a more sympathetic press nowadays. Not surprisingly, this patronizing approach infuriated most serious railway modellers of the day, and as a result they were at pains to stress the amount of craftsmanship that went into the production of scale models. One result of this is that operating a model

railway has been more associated with 'playing trains' and not been given the same regard, awe and respect granted to other aspects of the hobby.

This has been exacerbated by one very significant fact, namely that it is nowhere near as easy to put over the finer points of operating in a magazine as it is, for example, to show the delights of scenic modelling. Into the bargain, during my 30-odd years as a magazine editor of *Railway Modeller* and *Model Railways*, I found a great reluctance on the part of many operators to put pen to paper and explain

Gauge 1 NER 'R1' class 4-4-0 at the head of a typical train of teak coaches on the Gauge 1 Association's layout, seen at IMREX.

what they did. Current magazines suggest that this has not changed to any great extent in the past decade, yet articles on operation are always very popular. Fortunately, the growth of public exhibitions in the past 40 years has enabled many enthusiasts to discover the value of planned prototypical operation, not merely as a means of amusing the visitors, but also, far more to the point, as a way of preventing the operators going quietly mad over a three-day show.

At this point we must look at the fundamental difference between the full-size prototype and a small-scale replica. The former is provided to move people, parcels and products from place to place; the latter's primary purpose is to provide pleasure for its owner. While to the great majority of serious railway modellers, a close simulation of full-size practice provides the greatest satisfaction, the fact remains that we all enjoy a certain amount of fun on suitable occasions. It is easy to deride some features that have been introduced from time to time. Of course giraffes that duck down to pass under bridges, vans that explode, and, going back to the formative years before the First World War, coaches that in a collision disintegrate and disperse injured passengers around the trackside have enjoyed a brief flutter before passing into the oblivion that awaits most gimmicks dreamed up by over-imaginative sales directors. Yet most of us have a liking for the off-beat and bizarre, and I think it is a pity that we allow so much liberty to the well-meaning and earnest but essentially unimaginative critics, who love to pounce on and destructively criticize any feature they think not in accordance with prototype practice.

The fact is that some very odd things have happened on the full-size railways. For a start, every one of the original *Thomas the Tank Engine* stories had a basis in fact. I can't speak of the latest: there is no longer any need to read them. Yet if you look around you can see some apparently impossible situations. Let me give an example. About the only unencumbered place on most model railways is the station platform, so it is common practice to park defective vehicles here while reforming the train. One day I pointed out that while it made good sense to do this, on exhibition layouts such vehicles should be removed before the public are admitted. Sure enough, a week after publication, I received a

North Eastern Railway 'M1' class 4-4-0 at the head of a train of six-wheeled coaches on Wally Mayhew's finescale 7 mm layout.

photograph of a prototype tank wagon that had been parked on the end of a platform after a derailment.

Indeed, it is possible to find prototype justification for almost anything. Even the basic train set oval, devoid of points, on which it is only possible to exchange rolling stock by lifting it off the track, is not without full-size precedent, since in its original form the Glasgow Subway consisted of a double track oval without turnouts, but provided with a large hole surmounted by a crane to lift stock up into the workshops. This line also only lined and lettered one side of the stock. The other faced the tunnel walls and was given a plain coat of paint.

However, the fact that something is done on the prototype does not necessarily make it suitable for a model railway. This applies in particular force when the principle of modelling a tiny slice of the prototype is taken to extremes. Even today the prototype abounds with small stations and other features that appear to be ideally suited for true-to-scale modelling. Looked at as constructional exercises they are superb, but there what I have termed the 'Heckmondwyke' principle is involved, for as the pioneering P4 exhibition layout demonstrated so clearly, if you make an accurate model of a station where very little happens and then operate it strictly in accordance with prototype practice, very little happens on the model. 'Heckmondwyke' was a superb model and the trains were operated correctly. It was just that, as any experienced trainspotter knows, you don't go to a small passing station on a secondary route if you want to see action. At an exhibition visitors want to see action, whether they are only there to keep the kids happy or are serious modellers.

Model railway operation has three basic themes. The simplest is merely watching the trains go by. This is the essence of the basic train set oval, but with refinements it can be extremely effective and is employed to good effect in well-organized exhibition tail-chasers. Unfortunately, to do this properly requires a fair amount of space. The second theme is station operation, the formation and remarshalling of trains, deployment of locomotives, simulation of loading and unloading. This is particularly suited to limited spaces and is most commonly seen in the justly popular terminus-fiddle yard layout. The third is the most obvious, the operation of a complete system to a timetable.

The three themes should not be regarded as mutually exclusive. Indeed it is perfectly possible to build a layout on which all may be enjoyed to the full. It is more or less taken for granted that a terminus-fiddle yard system should be operated in accordance with an organized schedule, and that although it is often necessary to mount the fiddle yard directly against the station throat, the model is greatly improved if there is a length of unencumbered track, the main line, where the train can be seen moving against model scenery. As always, the amount of space that can be given over to any one theme is limited by overall resources. This does not necessarily mean a lavish supply of money, since Peter Denny's 'Buckingham' has incorporated all three themes to the full from its inception as a modest-size portable layout that lived in a flat.

I have often spoken of 'Buckingham' and held it up as an example to emulate, not because of its excellence as a model, excellent though it is, but because whatever approach to the hobby one wishes to describe, the layout shows how effective that particular approach can be when taken as part of a fully balanced concept. Operation has always been a keynote. From the

Bulleid West Country 'Pacific' at the head of a train of BR Mk 1 standard coaches on a large N gauge layout.

outset the trains have run to a timetable, and additions have been made and alterations carried out to the loco stud, rolling stock and infrastructure in order to enhance operation. A rake of coaches is built to provide stock for a new express train, which in turn would need a new locomotive. Even the construction of a manor house brought in its wake the redefinition of the train services to the nearby station that would follow, in the Edwardian period, from such an establishment.

When a model railway is operated to a properly conceived schedule, it comes to life. This applies as much to a simple system built from sectional track and completely devoid of scenery as it does to the most accurate finescale model of an actual stretch of railway, complete down to the prototype point rodding and signal wires. Indeed, if for any reason the model cannot be run in a realistic fashion, it can only be regarded as a developed train set, an overgrown toy, since it fails to follow the most significant feature of the prototype, moving people,

parcels and products from one place to another.

Of course we are all playing trains, but as in any other activity you play according to the rules. To a large extent, you can adapt the rules to suit yourself. The important thing is to be consistent within your own parameters, rather than to strive to follow prototype practice in every respect. Our model world doesn't conform precisely to the full-size original. We are, for example, as far off as ever from having passengers load themselves into our trains. On the other hand, our open wagons can be guaranteed a load! Not all aspects of prototype operation need to be followed, though most have been copied by someone. There is even the case where someone has risen from the dinner table to run the 7.15 train.

Or is there? I happen to know one of the individuals who is alleged to do this, but I've never known him to do so in my presence. He does, however, have a very subtle sense of humour, and I'd not put it past him gently to lead someone along the

Great Central Altrincham *2-4-0T heads a train of six-wheeled coaches into 'Grandborough Junction' on Peter Denny's EM gauge 'Buckingham'.*

trackside path, particularly if that someone is prone to lay down the law as to the one and only way to run a model railway according to the book, and is asking to be taken down a peg or two as a result.

CHAPTER 2
The train is the key

It is possible to operate a model railway with just one basic type of train, but this can get more than a trifle monotonous, as the working pattern lacks variety. It is best when there are several different types of train on the layout. To a very considerable extent the layout design has a bearing on this, since one needs to provide the facilities for handling a wide variety of trains. But before we can decide what facilities are needed, it is essential to determine the type of trains one is going to have on the layout.

Modern British prototype practice has severely reduced the different types of train on offer. Even privatization will, at the outset at all events, only provide different liveries for existing stock and some rearrangement of

the interiors; the operating pattern will remain much as it is today. In the golden days of steam there was ample variety, and so we will deal with the classic steam railway scene as it was from around 1890 to 1960.

At first sight, railway traffic divides neatly into two classes, passenger and freight. The hybrid mixed train, where goods wagons were attached behind a passenger coach or coaches, was little used in Britain. This was due to the Board of Trade's distrust of the system which, when most goods wagons were loose coupled and without continuous brakes, had some justification. Mixed trains did feature on some branches and were fairly common on light railways. As far as the timetable was concerned, they were treated as a

The Royal Scot *in 4 mm scale, headed by a Stanier 'Duchess' class Pacific.*

Express and freight. Western Region Warship BB diesel hydraulic hauling a train of BR Mk I stock passes a WR '94xx' class 0-6-0PT on a local goods train on Alan Smith's TT gauge layout.

passenger train that could convey freight, not as a different type of unit.

Goods trains are more readily dealt with than passenger services, since despite the varied make-up of the trains, the categories were more clearcut. There were just three types of goods train; the long-distance service that took entire train loads between marshalling or concentration yards, the local goods or pick-up, which delivered and collected wagons along its leisurely run, and the trip or transfer working, where blocks of wagons were moved a couple of miles to a marshalling yard, usually from a major

Goods train behind North Eastern Railway 0-6-0 passing through 'Ravensbeck' on the Keighley 7 mm Scale Group's exhibition layout. On the right rear, just behind the signal, a gas tank wagon used to fill the reservoirs on gas-lit coaches can be seen, whilst a bogie milk van with slatted sides stands in the goods shed road. In the bay on the left is an NER auto train headed by an 0-4-4T.

customer — for example a colliery, steelworks or large factory — or between two adjacent marshalling yards in a conurbation. Mostly the trains were assembled from a range of wagons, with standard open wagons and vans predominating, but there were some block trains that were made up from a single class of wagon for delivery of a specific load.

In steam days, the mainstay of most rail freight was coal in wagonloads. It is difficult today to realize just how important coal was in the British economy. Until the 1950s it was the principal source of heat, light and power, though this was becoming less the case as electricity and gas became the preferred local source.

Before 1939, a great deal of coal was delivered in privately owned wagons, the property either of coal merchants or large concerns that needed coal in wagonloads. There were two reasons for this. The first was that the private owner could keep his wagons on site for as long as he needed without incurring a hire charge, or demurrage as it is technically known. The second was to overcome the shortage of company wagons available for coal traffic. This arose partly from a reluctance to expend more scarce capital than was absolutely necessary, principally because once used for coal, the wagon could not carry other produce.

The majority of British coal wagons were four-wheeled, without continuous brakes, and provided with side doors plus, on occasions, end doors or, in even rarer cases, bottom doors. To distinguish these last two types, the company wagons were marked with symbols: a diagonal bar for end doors and a central V for bottom doors (side doors, obviously, were apparent to the casual observer). These markings are shown in typical form in Figure 1. They fell into disuse in the post-war period and were rarely seen on private

This train of high-capacity hopper coal wagons is typical of North Eastern Railway Central division (the former Stockton & Darlington) practice. So for that matter is the elegant 0-6-0 goods locomotive that heads it past 'Leasingthorne' on the 4 mm scale layout of F. Warren.

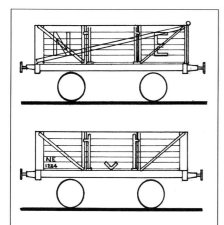

Figure 1 *Door markings on open wagons.*
Top: End door diagonal white line (latterly at a steeper angle from top corner to bottom of side door).
Bottom: Bottom doors.

owner wagons. The old North Eastern Railway, however, used large numbers of hopper wagons, while the GWR introduced and promoted a longer steel-bodied wagon with higher capacity. However, the standard 16 ft long wagon remained the favoured vehicle, largely because the various coal handling equipment up and down the country was built to handle wagons of this type.

In addition to the wagons used for general coal trade, all railway companies had their own fleet of coal wagons used to supply their locomotive depots, and these were normally branded LOCO. While other types of open wagon were used, it is advisable on any layout having a coaling stage to provide at least one LOCO coal wagon.

General merchandise was carried in open wagons and closed vans, the latter being used for the more valuable freight. In addition there were a large number of special-purpose wagons. The most common was the cattle wagon, for until the 1950s, a large pro-

portion of cattle for slaughter was carried by rail. This traffic only ceased when regulations were introduced requiring frequent watering and feeding. This had the effect of transferring the entire traffic from rail, where it was possible to carry out checks, to the road, where it is much more difficult. Cattle traffic was normally handled from separate loading platforms, provided with railed pens; the cattle dock or cattle loading was a prominent feature in most steam age goods yards.

Specialized wagons are good fun, but they need to be chosen with care, since unless you can justify their presence on the layout, they serve little purpose in serious operation. Obviously, when one is modelling a through station on a main line or cross-country route, there is considerable scope for including special wagons and their loads into the make-up of a 20-plus wagon train. It is a different matter on the pick-up goods. It would, for example, be a trifle difficult to explain why a propeller wagon should be run, with or without its load, along a line that does not serve a port.

Passenger stock divides into two broad categories, loco-hauled and multiple unit, these then being sub-divided according to their internal fittings. There is also a smudged area of push-pull fitted stock. These are in effect loco-hauled stock provided with a driving trailer and through communication to control the locomotive. In the steam era this practice was confined to short trains on local services. Today both the east and west coast electrified routes operate their principal services in this fashion.

Passenger trains also fall into two broad categories, the long-distance express and the short-distance local/commuter train. Current British Rail policy has gone as far as to separate them into different operating groups, the former being classed as

Express and Local. North London 0-6-0T and train of close-coupled four-wheel coaches is passed by an LNER express headed by an Ivatt 'Atlantic' on Geoff Bigmore's 'Bigston to Archway' 7 mm scale garden layout.

InterCity, the latter either as Regional Railways or Network South-East. However, as NSE operates many long-distance services that are by every other definition express trains — the Waterloo–Southampton–Weymouth service is the most obvious example — once again we have blurring between categories. Whatever the arguments might be for this broad differentiation on the prototype, on the model we have good reason to sub-divide still further.

We begin with the local train, one that stops at most if not all stations. At one end of this scale we have the regular, close-interval suburban train, heavily used by commuter traffic, often with eight or more coaches. At the other end we find the branch line shuttle, possibly one coach long, spending the entire day running to and from the terminus and the junction. In between there was the cross-country local, very much a steam age feature. It was usually between four and six coaches in length, often hauled by a tender engine rather than a tank locomotive and, in latter years, made up of older corridor coaches. All stations local services still exist on Regional Railways, providing feeder services to the limit-

ed stop express InterCity routes. These trains are today largely provided by diesel multiple unit stock (DMUs).

With express services, current practice is to operate these at regular intervals with a standard pattern of intermediate stops. Where a traditional name is used, it is applied to a specific timing rather than to a special set of stock. There is much to be said for this approach on the prototype, where any train is as good — or as bad — as any other. However, in the steam age things were different. Not only were timings haphazard, but there was a distinction between the principal expresses, almost invariably named trains, and the semi-fast trains that made up the bulk of the services and served more intermediate stations. Furthermore, the principal trains were usually made up from superior stock. This was not quite as wasteful as it appeared, since trains were much slower so that the special could only perform, at best, one round trip per day, while the Anglo-Scottish expresses managed just one journey in a working day.

When we translate this into model form, we encounter an interesting situation. A regular interval suburban service can easily be maintained by a single rake of coaches and two or three tank locomotives, or in later days by a diesel railcar set. However, in a steam age or early diesel era model we apparently require several main line trains, since each service had a distinctive make-up. This is where much depends on the storage capacity of the model, a subject I will return to in later chapters. In the early stages of the layout's life, the amount of equipment on hand also has an important bearing on train make-up, but this is a temporary situation and need not affect long-term planning.

One convenient solution to the problem of stock shortage is to add a strengthening coach to a standard set of stock, thus altering the character of the train. Let us assume there is just room for a five-coach train on the layout. A basic set of four coaches, brake second, first, and two second class coaches constitutes the core. In this form it is essentially a cross-country local set. Add a restaurant car and it becomes an express. Replace the restaurant car with a sleeping car and you have an overnight service. A Royal Mail van makes it into a postal train, while a parcels van turns it into a newspaper train. At the same time, different classes of locomotive would be put on to the train to help change its identity. Figure 2 shows this in diagrammatic form, and how the extra vehicle might be located in the set. A great deal will depend on where and how the extra coach is added to the train. If it is done in station limits there is ample opportunity for additional shunting, but sufficient provision is needed for storing the spare coaches. Alternatively, the extra coach can be added by hand in a fiddle yard or storage sidings.

This is only the start. There are many specialized freight vehicles that are not only fitted with continuous brakes, but also have running gear suitable for express passenger speeds. These vehicles are frequently referred to as passenger rated stock. While many of these are to be found in express freight services, they could be

Typical Great Western branch trains. In the foreground an ex-Taff Vale 0-6-2T is waiting to haul a pair of Dean period non-corridor clerestory coaches, whilst in the bay road beyond a '14xx' 0-4-2T is coupled to a standard auto-trailer coach.

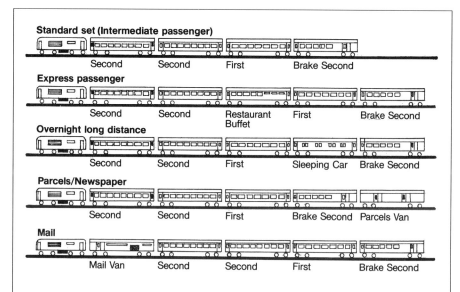

Figure 2 *Varied passenger trains produced by adding a strengthening coach to a basic rake.*

attached to passenger trains, though this practice is far less common today.

While this shuffling about appears fussy, in practice it adds interest to the working of the principal station if you have to alter the make-up of a passenger train from time to time. Further interest is provided by parcels traffic that is often handled in the passenger section of the station.

This is no more than a condensed outline of the main possibilities, but I hope I have said enough to whet the appetite. Although we resent having our model railway described as a train set, we should never lose sight of the fact that the trains are the most important feature of our layouts, and that although you are moving away from the concept of a toy, operating your trains realistically and arranging their make-up to conform with full-size practice is a very important part of the fun.

CHAPTER 3
Station working

The disappearance from Britain of the pick-up goods and the change from loco-hauled to multiple unit stock has taken away one of life's little pleasures, leaning on the railway fence watching the working of a busy station. This is not the inevitable result of modern traction, for one can still see plenty of interesting station working in Switzerland, where electric traction has been the rule for over half a century. However, we are straying from our main theme. No matter what has happened on the prototype, we can still operate our model stations in the old-fashioned way. It's more fun than standing by the present day railway fence.

Station working is probably the most important aspect of model railway operation. This is not to suggest it is intrinsically superior to full timetable working of an extensive system by a group of friends, for this is demonstrably not so. Its importance lies in the fact that it is within the grasp of a lone enthusiast hampered by restricted space and limited resources. At the same time, the majority of layouts

Shunting in progress on Alan Wright's second 'Inglenook Sidings', first seen at the 1992 Manchester Model Railway Society's annual exhibition. An LNER 'J72' 0-6-0T is the motive power. Like the wagons it is a standard commercial product. Each wagon is of a distinctive design so that there can be no mistake in the ordering of the train.

worked to a timetable also enjoy the delights of station working.

An elaborate, complex network of points and crossings is not necessary, since some fascinating shunting can be carried out in very simple stations. Indeed, two turnouts, correctly arranged, can, in a very limited space indeed, provide one with an enjoyable little shunting yard, as shown in Figure 3. At first sight it seems far too simple to provide any real interest, but in practice it can be quite taxing.

In addition to the layout itself, you need one shunting locomotive, steam or diesel, which should be a good reliable slow runner, and between eight and twelve different wagons, each easily identifiable. Auto-couplings are to be preferred, and need to be in good working order, properly adjusted so that coupling and uncoupling is completely dependable. For each wagon, you will also need a card with the identity of the vehicle clear-

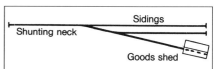

Figure 3 *Simple shunting yard. This three-track formation is the basis of most model station goods yards.*

ly set out on one side.

First of all, you determine the maximum length of train you can pull clear of the first turnout on to the shunting neck. Four wagons are about right for this small yard. Shuffle the cards and deal out four, then set about assembling a train with the four wagons in the order of dealing. This is not quite as easy as it looks. The more wagons you have, and the less free room on each siding, the more difficult it becomes to get the end wagon in one siding on to the front end of the train.

This arrangement dates back to 1926, when A.R. Walkley described his

Passing loop in action on Alan Wright's 'Cheviotdale'. The passenger train, an 'N2' 0-6-2T, a vacuum-fitted van for parcels traffic and a pair of LNER panelled teak-bodied corridor coaches, has been waiting in the platform road for the arrival of the branch goods, headed by an ex-North Eastern 'J25' 0-6-0 in LNER black livery.

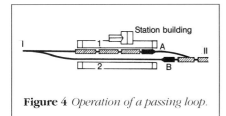

Figure 4 *Operation of a passing loop.*

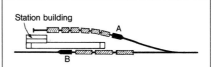

Figure 5 *Passing trains with a lie-by siding.*

railway in a suitcase, but its popularity began when Alan Wright first showed 'Inglenook Sidings' to visitors to the Manchester MRS Exhibition in the 1970s. Since then this little scheme has been copied time and time again. It makes an ideal first exercise in serious model railway construction, and as it will go into the recess beside the chimney breast — hence the name — it will fit into most homes. It is also an excellent device for learning the fine art of shunting a goods yard, a very important part of serious model railway operation.

A very important train manoeuvre on both prototype and model is the passing of two trains travelling in opposite directions on a single line route. This normally requires a passing loop, shown in Figure 4. The arrangement is obvious. Train A arrives in road 1 from section I and waits for train B to enter road 2 from Section II. Optionally, since section I is clear, train B can proceed through the station without stopping.

An alternative situation is shown in Figure 5, where there is a lie-by siding, into which train A is backed to

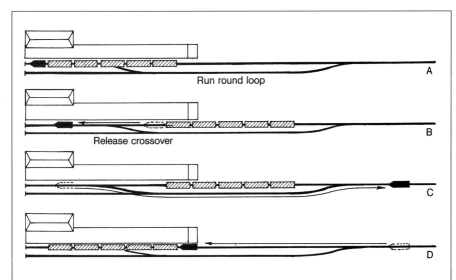

Figure 6 *Operation of a run-round loop.*
A: Train arrives in station.
B: Train is backed fully on to the loop; locomotive pulls forward clear of release crossover.
C: Locomotive runs round train using loop line.
D: Locomotive backs on to train, couples, then pushes coaches back into platform.

Figure 7 *Run-round loop beyond platforms. In this arrangement, the one loop serves three platform roads, a considerable economy in track and points.*

allow Train B to pass. In this instance, train A would normally not be carrying passengers, mainly because of regulations, but also because passengers take a dim view of such proceedings.

An equally important set of basic movements concerns the reversal of locomotive-hauled stock at termini. The basic system, often regarded by railway modellers as the main one, is to provide a run-round loop. The function is shown in Figure 6. The train arrives in the platform and either stops with the leading vehicle clear of the fouling point of the release crossover, or is backed into this position. The locomotive is then uncoupled and runs forward, the release crossover and the entry point into the loop are reversed, and the locomotive runs back around

its train. The loop entry point and release crossover are returned to normal and the locomotive backs on to the train that it pushes back to the end of the platform. Although the clearance between the end stops and the release crossover need not be longer than the largest locomotive to use the station, it is very useful to have enough room to have a parcels van parked against the buffers so that it can be coupled to the rear of the appropriate train.

The loop need not be adjacent to the platform. If it is further out, as in Figure 7, it will serve not only the main platform but also the bay road. This also allows a set of coaches to stand in both platform roads while the goods yard is being shunted and the freight train prepared for departure. The only

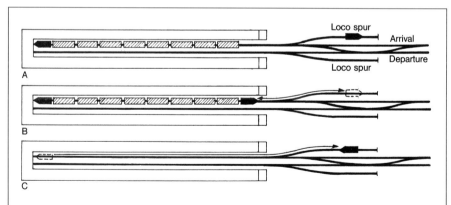

Figure 8 *Reversing a train using a spare locomotive.*
A: Train arrives, locomotive uncouples. Spare locomotive waiting in loco spur.
B: Spare locomotive backs on to coaches, couples and becomes train locomotive, waits for departure signal.
C: After train leaves, the original train locomotive, now spare, backs into loco spur and waits for the next arrival.

snag is that this does take up a good deal of space, unless the loop is carried around the inevitable curve leading to the terminus. This arrangement is very convenient for the more impressive main line type of station with three or more platform faces.

However, at main line stations it is customary to employ additional locomotives. In the most straightforward arrangement, mainly though not exclusively employed for local services, the spare locomotive waits in a short spur ready to back on to the train and take it out again. Once the train has departed, the original train engine backs into the loco spur to await the next arrival. This is shown in Figure 8. In the diesel era, this arrangement is used to reverse all passenger trains, since diesels (and electric locomotives) need little servicing and definitely do not need to be turned.

Steam age long-distance semi-fast and express trains were handled differently. Probably the most interesting arrangement involves separate arrival and departure platforms. As shown in Figure 9, the train arrives and a station shunter couples up at the rear, pulling the coaches clear and releasing the train engine which then proceeds to the locomotive depot. I'll deal with this aspect of steam age working in more detail further into this chapter, and in the meantime we will concentrate on the coaches. In the diagram, there is a separate shunting road long enough to take the train and the station shunter. The coaches are drawn into this track before being pushed into another platform, the departure road.

This is an interesting manoeuvre which can be further developed if sufficient room is available for a set of carriage sidings. This allows a rake of

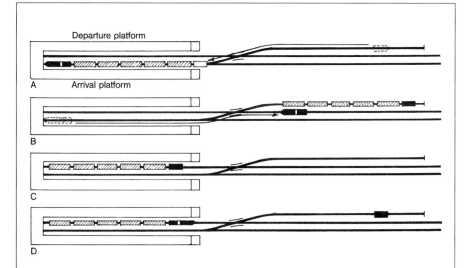

Figure 9 *Express train reversal with arrival and departure platforms.*
A: Express in arrival road, shunter attached to back.
B: Shunter draws coaches into long siding. Train locomotive backs out and proceeds to loco depot for coal, water and turning.
C: Shunter pushes coaches into departure platform.
D: Shunter returns to siding. Train engine, duly turned on turntable, backs on to coaches, couples and is ready to depart.

coaches to be held over for some time. In former times, the coaches would frequently be taken to the carriage sidings for a thorough clean internally, and possibly externally as well, while the header tanks in the lavatories were refilled. With modern trains this is less prevalent, the tanks being replenished from bowsers on the platforms. On some smaller termini, hoses were provided between platform roads for this purpose.

As an alternative, the coaches can be pushed into the carriage sidings by the train engine before it heads off for the depot. The shunter then pulls the coaches into the platform, where it remains trapped until the train departs.

It is also possible to reverse an express passenger train by attaching a fresh locomotive to the rear of the train. This is very much the case where diesel and electric traction is involved. It is particularly attractive on a model since it provides a good reason for having rather more large tender locomotives than are strictly necessary.

Steam locomotives required a lot of attention. They consumed prodigious quantities of water — most of the exhaust was in fact steam — and burned anything up to 10 tons of coal in a shift, which consequently produced a couple of tons of ash, mainly in the ashpan. A fair amount was also left in the smokebox, even with the self-cleaning smokebox that ejected as much unburnt material as possible out of the chimney and on to the surrounding landscape. Hence in steam days, there was markedly less undergrowth around the tracks than there is today, and from summer until spring large burned patches could be seen on embankments and cutting sides.

Locomotives were serviced at regular depots as well as at smaller installations close to stations, while water cranes were provided on the platforms of most important stations so that the tender or side tanks could be refilled. Above all, tender locomotives normally required turning at the end of their runs, since the old Board of Trade and its successor, the Ministry of Transport, considered that tender-first running was potentially dangerous. However, it was practised on some branches and on routes that were provided with locomotives fitted with backplates or rudimentary cabs on the tenders. Locomotive crews would turn engines whenever possible. Tender-first driving was extremely uncomfortable at anything above a crawl, since coal dust was blown back into the cab, making working conditions almost intolerable.

When large-capacity tenders came into general use on larger locomotives, the further problem of the lack of anything approaching a clear rear view also played its part. This meant that locomotive handling facilities were needed at all major stations, and a small selection of different arrangements are depicted in Figure 10. We start with what can best be described as valeting fittings, locations where locomotives could have their essential needs catered for. In example A we are down to basics, a pit between the rails into which the contents of the ashpan could be emptied. This was essential, since if ash was allowed to accumulate it reduced the flow of primary air to the fire, impairing the steaming and, in extreme cases, killing the fire. Fresh coal was to hand on a platform, and was put into the bunker by basket. It was hard work, and occasionally a hand-operated crane would be provided. Alongside would be a large water column to replenish the tanks. This had a large bore and could discharge several thousand gallons in a few minutes. To supply this demand, water was stored in a high-level header tank which was invariably located fairly close to the standpipes to reduce the length of large bore piping needed.

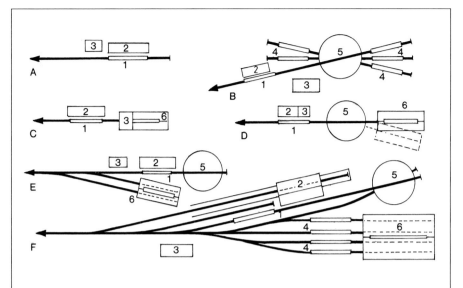

Figure 10 *Locomotive depot arrangements. For details, see text.*
Key:
1 Ashpit; 2 Coal stage; 3 Water tank; 4 Inspection pit; 5 Turntable; 6 Locomotive shed.

At B we have a larger valeting depot, as might be found near a main line terminus. Here a turntable provides access to a number of radial roads, each provided with an inspection pit. This was provided so that the locomotive crew could get underneath to inspect and oil the inside motion of older inside-cylindered machines, as well as the larger multi-cylinder types. This type of yard was provided in addition to the main locomotive depot which might be a mile or more down the line. It was mainly used by visiting locomotives; those allocated to the station's depot would normally return there, since their arrival was usually arranged to coincide with the end of the shift.

At C we have a very small installation with a shed, typical of the branch terminus. The water tank is mounted above the shed, a configuration more popular on models than it was on the prototype where it was usually adopted where space was limited — which is why it is so popular among modellers. Another space-saving dodge was to mount the tank over the coal stage. There was ample room for coal under the tank, and this is shown at D, where a turntable is included. On most branches this would be a relatively small unit, 50 to 55 ft in diameter and only capable of turning a 4-4-0 or 2-6-0 tender engine. The shed was normally situated beyond the turntable, since during the day it would be empty. It is possible to angle the shed road as shown in dotted lines, as was done at Swanage. It is of great help on a compact model as it allows a shed to be tucked into a corner. These sheds would incorporate an inspection pit and a workbench, and frequently had a lean-to bothy where the engine crew could brew up and deal with any paperwork in comparative comfort.

These depots were sub-sheds, providing overnight storage for the branch locomotive, eliminating the need to send it out from the main shed some

Basic locomotive facilities are provided at this model sub-shed on Geraint Hughes' model based on the Cromford & High Peak section of the LMS. The water tank is clearly in its second (or could it be third?) incarnation, mounted on a simple frame and provided with a direct discharge to replenish the locomotive's tanks. The tiny coal stage is no more than a small stone platform to hold a heap of coal; the bothy behind began life as a brake van. Ash is shovelled out on to the track and loaded into a wagon when convenient. The brick-built shed is easily the most substantial part of the sub-shed.

hours before it was due to begin work. This also meant that the locomotive crew could live in the town and walk or cycle to work. This was, and for that matter still is, a significant consideration, since railwaymen need to get to work before anyone else can go about their business. Only limited maintenance facilities were provided at sub-sheds, any major overhauls or repairs being carried out at the main motive power depot.

At E we have a somewhat larger sub-shed, with covered storage for two locomotives, and the turntable and valeting facilities on a third road, whilst in F we can see what, in model terms, passes for a motive power depot.

The configuration is based on the GWR design evolved in the 1890s. The shed has four tracks and is capable, just, of holding eight locomotives under cover with a further four stabled outside. Inspection pits are provided inside the shed and outside in the standing area. The coaling stage has its own wagon road, raised to enable the coal to be shovelled into skips which were used to tip coal into the tenders or bunkers below. A siding alongside the ashpit was provided for the wagons that carried the ash away to a tipping site.

A locomotive would come 'on shed' at the end of a shift and stand over the ashpit to clear the ashpan and smokebox, taking on water at the same time. Then it proceeded to the coal stage where the fuel supply was replenished, before moving on to the turntable where it would be turned end for end. Meantime other engines would have joined the queue, so a second turntable road was provided to allow the replenished locomotive to move off. It might set back on shed, or alternatively set off on another tour of duty.

This is not a full motive power

depot, which would also include a couple of storage roads, one of which was generally occupied by the breakdown crane and tool vans. Another road was occupied with locomotives awaiting repair: the cripple road. An MPD would often incorporate a further shed fitted out with a small array of machine tools, including a wheel lathe, together with one or more often two large travelling hoists capable of lifting a boiler off the frames. This workshop was used for minor repairs and intermediate overhauls, but could strip a locomotive into its component parts and rebuild it if need be. Only boiler work was outside its scope. Even when there was no separate workshop, the MPD would have a set of sheer legs or other hoist to allow a locomotive to be lifted clear of its wheels so that a very common fault, the hot box, where for one reason or another, a main wheel bearing became

overheated and worn, could be attended to. This facility was also needed to allow wheels to be removed and sent away for reprofiling.

It will be seen that a complete steam age locomotive depot was a large and complex affair. A thoroughgoing model will take up a good deal of space, but because so much of the working is self-contained, it is perfectly possible to make this the entire layout. It is a particularly attractive theme for the modeller who either builds or collects locomotive models, since a median-sized shed would have 40 or more locomotives allocated to it, and be visited, in the course of a day, by as many again.

We have already touched on shunting. It is important to realize that in the steam age there were two classes of freight yards, the normal goods yards and the marshalling or concentration yards. The latter were used solely for

North London inside-cylindered 4-4-0T heading out from Geoff Bigmore's 'Bigston' at the head of a close-coupled set of North London four-wheeled coaches.

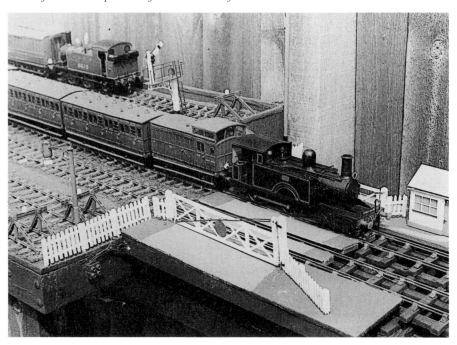

The train arrives at the high-level terminus 'Westbridge'. This is a very basic affair and consists of a length of track alongside a platform with a short locomotive spur at the approach end.

sorting wagons into trains for various destinations and were accordingly very large indeed, and, while an extremely fascinating feature, can only be accommodated on an extensive layout, or occupy the entire layout in their own right. Shunting went on six days a week, 24 hours a day, with powerful floodlights or, in early days, arc lights for illumination after dark.

The North London outside-cylindered 0-6-0T which was waiting in the spur now backs on to the other end of the set of coaches. As on the prototype, a short guard's van with a raised look-out is coupled at each end of the train.

The train is now awaiting the signal to leave 'Westbridge'. Meantime, on the low-level main line, a Gresley quad-art high-capacity articulated suburban set passes behind a condensing 'N2' 0-6-2T, the standard motive power for the Great Northern London suburban lines.

Goods yards are the point where freight is transhipped. As a result, shunting by locomotive only took place at fixed times, frequently early in the morning or late at night so that the local traders could load and unload their merchandise. Movement of wagons at other times was either by horse or by hand. The old 16 ton four-wheeled wagon could be moved by three men and kept rolling by one, or alternatively a pinch bar expertly applied to one wheel got things moving. In larger yards, capstans were provided for rope shunting. However, spotting individual wagons by means of the forefinger is not regarded as sound model railway operating practice.

Industrial sidings were similar to the goods yard. In model form it is rarely practicable to lay down an extensive network, unless the industrial network is the whole of the layout. However, many yards owned small locomotives and did their own shunting, and an industrial offshoot makes for an interesting addition to a moderately sized station complex, scenically and operationally, since the rigid rules applying to public railways could be largely ignored on private premises where the Ministry of Transport's writ did not run.

Station working involves a good deal of coupling and uncoupling. Automatic couplings are not a necessity, and many people are perfectly happy to use prototypical three-link couplings. Paradoxically this trend is more common amongst finescale modellers, and in particular those who are fussy to a hundredth of a millimetre — on paper at least — but seem oblivious to the introduction of an overscale hand wielding an elongated shunter's pole. We all have our blind spots, I suppose.

In 7 mm scale, three-link couplings are the norm, though a few exhibition operators use auto couplings with considerable success. It is worth pointing out that the seminal 7 mm scale exhibition layout, Bill Banwell's 'Maybank', which I saw at the 1939 Model Railway Exhibition, employed automatic

Basic goods facilities, a fairly large shed spanning a single track. A small hand-operated crane is provided to lift heavy loads off wagons and on to a waiting road vehicle. This model is based on the old Hornby-Dublo OO gauge system, using flexible track with added centre conductor rail. Scratch-built structures are employed to provide a more authentic picture. The freight train is, somewhat improbably, headed by a 'Castle' class 4-6-0 and includes two Peco Wonderful wagons. It also has a brake van at the front as well as one at the back. Whilst unlikely to be seen in full size, this dodge enables a fixed train of wagons to be run back and forth with reasonable fidelity to prototype practice.

couplings to avoid the intrusion of hands into the modelled scene. Going to the other extreme, most N gauge operators use the standard auto coupling.

In OO gauge many modellers are perfectly content with the tension lock coupling provided on most OO gauge ready-to-run British stock. This coupling is a development of the original design used by A.R. Walkley on his pioneer shunting yard, replacing the flimsy wire of the original with massive steel or plastic parts. Its action is shown in Figure 11. While the vehicles are being pulled and the coupling is in tension, the hooks engage with the loop and the sprung ramp is depressed by the lower extension of the hook. When the vehicles are being

pushed the hooks are disengaged and are lifted by the ramp, to drop back again afterwards. If the train is stopped and reversed with a coupling over the ramp, the train is split at this point. By locating an uncoupling ramp at the clearance point in each siding, remote shunting becomes a reasonably straightforward matter. Clearly the shunting locomotive needs to be fully responsive to control, and the operator must be able to see when the coupling is over the ramp.

Similar ramps can be located in platform roads where uncoupling needs to take place, as explained earlier in this chapter. This is fine in termini, but locating a sprung ramp in a running road can lead to unpredictable slip coach working. Ramps can be lowered

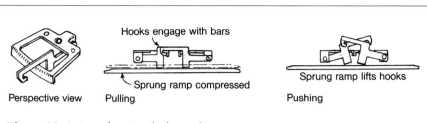

Figure 11 *Action of tension lock coupling.*

mechanically or raised by means of an electromagnet to get round this problem.

When pushing, the two curved faces of the loops engage and propel the vehicles, avoiding any problems with buffer locking on curves, albeit at the expense of over-scale spacing between vehicles.

The Peco Simplex coupling that was once popular through the now defunct Hornby Dublo system is still available. It provides a reasonable facsimile of a buckeye coupling, but is rather sensitive to uneven track. However, the coupling is reasonably unobtrusive and will propel vehicles around sharp curves without any difficulty. The latest pattern is magnetically operated, getting over the main difficulty with this excellent design, the fact that it does require a lifting ramp for reliable uncoupling.

There are several British specialized couplings, the best known and most widely used being the Sprat and Winkle supplied by Model Railway Signal Engineering. This is a much finer magnetically operated version of the tension lock, inverted and now arranged for advance uncoupling. Figure 12 shows how it operates. The non-magnetic etched hooks are provided with steel coupling links which are drawn down by the track-mounted magnet. For siding work a small permanent magnet is provided, while on running roads it is better to install electromagnets energized by a push button.

The bar is either fitted across the buffers or else incorporated into a mounting unit. The vehicle's buffers are now doing their proper job and therefore this coupling is not really suited for a layout with sharp reverse curves.

Advance uncoupling is a system whereby the coupling can be disengaged in advance whilst the train is

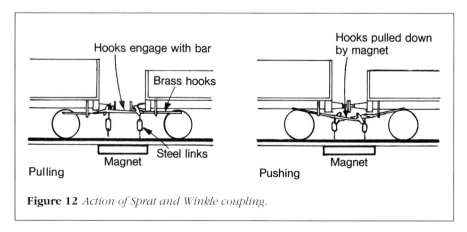

Figure 12 *Action of Sprat and Winkle coupling.*

being pushed. This allows the cut to be made anywhere along the siding, and it also means that a fan of sidings can be shunted with only one decoupling ramp. Like all advantages, it has its downside, and the shunting locomotive needs to be very smooth and slow-running, whilst the operator must be quick to press the button actuating the uncoupler.

Advance uncoupling is also offered by the Kaydee coupling, a device of US origin, and generally regarded as one of the best couplings available. It is a near-scale working model of a buckeye coupling, and despite its delicate appearance has proved to be both robust and reliable. It is not absolutely perfect, and does have two well-known snags: it is the most expensive coupling on the market, and it incorporates a minute compression spring that has to be fitted by the user. There is a very good reason why the pack contains several springs; they are apt to fly across the room and are virtually impossible to find once they hit the floor.

Another advance uncoupler is the AFJ. Unlike those previously mentioned, this is not a commercial product, but it is fairly easy for an experienced model maker to make in the home workshop from spring wire. Since its invention by Alex Jackson in the late 1940s, the design has been refined, and its construction has been detailed on many occasions in magazines. However, it is strictly for the advanced worker, since, like the girl in the poem, when it is good it is very very good, but when it is bad it is horrid.

On the Continent couplings fall into two patterns, the basic type originally developed by Märklin and the later variable distance patterns, which provide close coupling on the straight but stretch out on curves. These are available as spare parts, with some difficulty, and can be fitted to British products.

On the face of it, it might seem sensible to have one pattern coupling on the layout. In practice this is not necessary where a reasonably large loco stud is available and different locos can be equipped to take different couplings. However, this is really only acceptable under three special conditions. The first is where the decision has been taken to change from one pattern coupling to another. Clearly this cannot be done overnight and is best carried out on a train by train basis. The second is where a different coupling is used on freight stock to that on passenger, possibly having variable distance couplings on coaching stock, where over-wide spacing is most noticeable, and advance uncouplers on goods stock. The third case is where stock is assembled in fixed rakes and only provided with auto couplings at the ends.

Where this is done, it is common practice to employ a very old device that is no longer in production, the bar and pin coupling. This is nothing more than a length of strip metal, usually brass; for OO gauge 3 mm x 1 mm section is preferred. The extreme end has a small pin, with a hole immediately behind it. Figure 13 shows its construction and use. It is readily produced in the home workshop and,

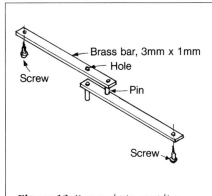

Figure 13 *Bar and pin coupling.*

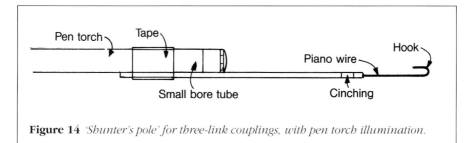

Figure 14 *'Shunter's pole' for three-link couplings, with pen torch illumination.*

unless very sloppily fitted, utterly reliable in use. In general, this coupling is used on coaches. Where wagons are assembled in rakes it is more common to use three-link couplings.

Three-link couplings are surprisingly popular among serious modellers. Providing one accepts the intrusion of the overscale hand and arranges matters so that operators can readily reach the vital parts of the layout, they have several undeniable virtues. First of all, they look right. Secondly, they rarely uncouple on their own. Thirdly, they do not require special ramps or magnets to make them work. Fourthly, they do not couple unless you deliberately place the loops over the coupling hook. Against this, they are perceived as being difficult to hook up. This is largely a matter of practice and of getting the right tool for the job. My own favourite is a simple shunter's pole, made from a length of fine bore tubing and a piece of piano wire. The assembly is shown in Figure 14. The wire is secured in the tube by pinching the side with a pair of pliers, and the end of the wire is bent into a loop. The drawing shows an optional extra: the tube is taped to a pen-torch to provide illumination between the vehicles.

Coupling under corridor connections on coaches is a very fiddly job, hence coach sets tend to remain in fixed rakes. Coupling beneath overall roofs at termini might seem impossible unless the roof is removed. However, one does not normally need to couple

trains, only detach the train engine. This can be done by means of a simple trip device on the locomotive, detailed in Figure 15. A dummy screw coupling is bent from wire and provided with a pair of lugs on either side of the hook. A sprung trip is placed in the track a little over the maximum locomotive length from the buffers. As the locomotive passes over this trip, the two lugs lift the coupling links off the hook, and they fall clear. Not only has the locomotive been detached from the train, but also the couplings will not re-engage.

Before we leave couplings, there are two very useful dodges and one essential factor worth bearing in mind. Whenever it is necessary to couple a pair of totally incompatible couplings, a piece of bent wire will usually do the trick — a paper clip is the traditional source. When, in the rough and tum-

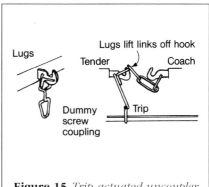

Figure 15 *Trip-actuated uncoupler for three-link couplings.*

ble of an exhibition, couplings show an annoying tendency to part company in the middle of a train, a small elastic band slipped over the working parts is a sovereign remedy. Alternatively, make use of the bent bit of wire! Last of all, the best auto coupling on earth will not work unless both mating parts are correctly aligned. When one is dealing with over a hundred couplings, as will be the case on anything but a very small layout, it is essential to have one fixed reference against which all couplings are set. This usually takes the form of a block of hardwood that sits on the track and

has a coupling fixed at the correct height.

Why are there so many different auto couplings in use? The answer is simple: no one coupling meets every need, new designs are launched at regular intervals, and the advent of etching makes this a practical proposition for a cottage industry. Unfortunately, cottage industries do cease trading from time to time, and therefore I have not mentioned several promising newcomers. Only time will tell if they will make the grade or disappear into the mist of time like the Lanal and Nucro.

CHAPTER 4
Design for operation

Designing a model railway, as opposed to drawing out a track plan, involves such matters as the type of trains you want to run, the sort of landscape through which you want them to run, the period and prototype you intend to follow and, above all, the method of operation you intend to follow. If you do not think of operation at the outset you can easily fall into a number of elementary traps, and while we will be considering in detail the various ways of operating a model railway realistically we need to begin by considering the situation in global terms.

First of all, let's deal with that awkward trap that is waiting for us at the

'Blacksanton' is typical of a station that provides plenty of scope for interesting operation. In addition to the up and down through roads, there is a bay platform, currently occupied by a GWR diesel railcar, which can provide not merely a convenient local service but can also disappear up a stub branch and return later to correspond with the layout's timetable. Behind the station is a commendably compact goods yard with adequate facilities for freight traffic. The pick-up goods has just arrived behind a '57xx' 0-6-0PT, which will shortly shunt the yard, leaving a couple of wagons and removing both empty and freshly loaded vehicles.

outset, modelling an actual prototype. As the original station was operated by a railway, clearly it must be capable of being operated prototypically when modelled faithfully. Unfortunately, although there were and still are a large number of stations small enough and simple enough to fit into a cramped site when modelled to scale, their train service was equally restricted. If anyone doubts this, then I suggest he visits St Ives in Cornwall and studies the present branch terminus, a single spur road alongside a platform, served by a railcar shuttling back and forth from St Erth. As a modelling project it would be admirable, since the setting is magnificent. As a fully automated exhibition feature it would have some merit, but as the basis for serious operation it has absolutely nothing to offer. There are other similar stations, where a branch has been reduced to a single track spur, but St Ives is well worth visiting in its own

right. The original steam worked terminus did have an interesting operating pattern and a very attractive layout.

The second trap is even more subtle. To use current jargon, operation involves a man/model interface. Put another way, someone has to be there to run the trains. What is more to the point, the operator needs to be fairly close to the action. Yes, you can operate points and drive trains from point to point over the layout from a remote centralized control panel, but you can't carry out uncoupling unless you are in the right position to see when the couplings are over the decoupling device, and when recoupling you need to be able to see what is happening when coupling is imminent. This means you must not only be within 2 metres at the outside, but you must also be broadside on to the tracks.

On a compact layout this doesn't arise, since one would need to be perverse to locate the controller in an

Plan 1 *Simple continuous layout.*
Key:
1 Station building; 2 Signal cabin; 3 Goods shed; 4 Locomotive shed.

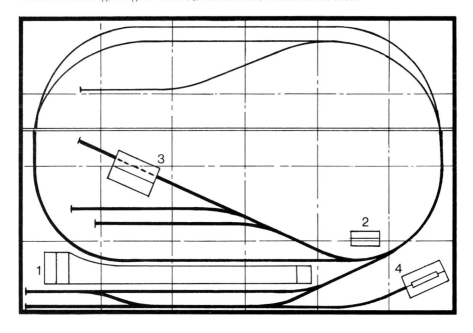

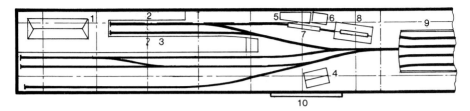

Plan 2 *Steam age branch terminus.*
Key:
1 Station building; 2 Cattle loading; 3 Bay and parcels road; 4 Signal cabin ; 5 Coal stage;
6 Water Tank; 7 Ashpit; 8 Locomotive shed; 9 4-track traverser; 10 Controls.

inconvenient position. If we look at the very elementary layout in Plan 1 it is clear that no matter where one stands, most of the layout is within easy reach and everything is in full view. This simple scheme illustrates the basic difficulty with small continuous layouts, namely that the operating pattern is extremely limited. The provision of hidden loops and a storage road behind a backscene allows one to accommodate three complete trains in comfort, but a fourth would make operation difficult. There is a reasonable-size goods yard and a terminal road with a run-round loop which will allow limited station working. Unfortunately, a single solid 6 ft x 4 ft baseboard is not the ideal basis for an operating layout. Dressed up with landscape and buildings, this could be a pleasing modelling project.

Plan 2 is the ever-popular steam age branch terminus, feeding a traverser fiddle yard. The latter will be fully explained in Chapter 7 while branches are dealt with in Chapter 9. This type of layout can be operated exactly in accordance with the prototype, but as most branches were operated by a shuttle service, using the same locomotive and pair of coaches, we tend to embellish the schedule. The four roads on the traverser will hold all the trains one can plausibly deploy.

The locomotive shed, with its full complement of facilities, is arranged

as a kickback from the road serving the cattle loading platform. It is not a good idea to take it off a bay road in this fashion, since for part of the time the bay will be full of parcels vans. It is one thing to add to the complexity of shunting, another thing altogether to invite gridlock. Controls are mounted behind the signal cabin for the obvious reason that this is the spot where most of the action takes place.

Although this plan allows prototypical working, operation is rather like a fisherman's walk, two steps and overboard. Turning to Plan 3, we have the excellent U-shaped terminus-fiddle yard scheme, which does provide a stretch of clear main line track where one can see the train gather speed before it plunges under the road overbridge into the fiddle yard. The yard is flanked by a model quayside line, with a line of low relief buildings masking the fiddle yard.

The loco depot has collected a turntable, and the shed is now run off the table at an angle. This is a crib from Swanage, though the angle is considerably greater than on that prototype. In this case the bay road has a long enough approach to avoid any risk of blocking the entry to the loco depot with a train. The coal siding faces the opposite way to the rest of the goods roads. This is a deliberate snarl introduced to make shunting a little more challenging.

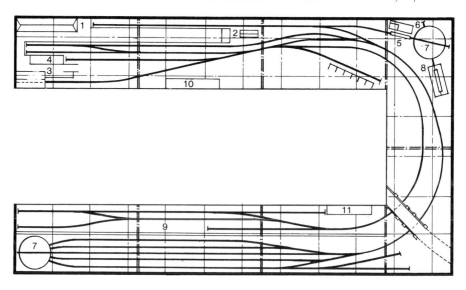

Plan 3 *U-shaped terminus-fiddle yard.*
Key:
1 Station building; 2 Signal cabin; 3 Goods shed; 4 Cattle loading; 5 Ashpit; 6 Coal stage with water tank; 7 Turntable; 8 Locomotive shed; 9 Low relief buildings; 10 Controls.

The quayside tracks are very much a steam age feature, but anyone wishing to see just how they might be arranged can study the remains of the Weymouth tramway. Although this line was closed to traffic on electrification, the rails remain in situ and can be readily followed on the ground. Whilst in Weymouth, make a visit to the Wellington Arms in St Alban Street.

This close-up view of 'Leasingthorne Colliery' reveals a lot of interesting detail; the boiler house for example. The chaldron wagons in the foreground are for internal use only, being quite unsuitable for main line use. One of the wagons has dumb buffers. These lingered for quite a while on the North Eastern railway, though by the period this scene is set — the early years of this century — they were being phased out as rapidly as possible.

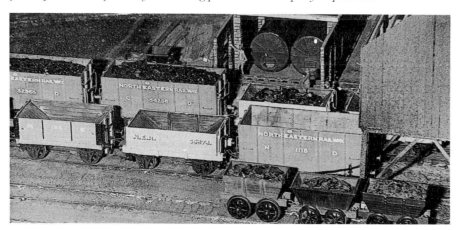

Even in the diesel era, freight working takes place, though there is ample evidence that this quarry scene is set in the late '60s or early '70s. The 'Peak' class 1-Co-Co-1 diesel is in green livery, the 08 0-6-0 shunter is now very much a museum piece (it had its beginnings in the steam age), whilst the presence of a GWR pattern goods brake and wooden-bodied wagons date the scene.

There are a couple of photos of the tramway in action showing just how many wagons used to line the quay.

It would be next-door to impossible to operate the quay roads and the fiddle yard from the main controls. They require their own control panel, but as the two boards are on opposite sides of a common operating well, it is just a matter of turning around as the train moves from one side of the layout to the other. With two panels there is the opportunity for two-operator working, therefore the operating positions are staggered.

Where a reasonably sized permanent site is available, there is more scope for interesting layout design, but it is all too easy to overlook the importance of operator convenience. Plan 4 shows how an interesting branch line out-and-back system can be fitted into a moderately large spare room, providing convenience for operation. The two main stations — the branch terminus and the junction station — are on opposite sides of a common operating well which is entered directly from the doorway. With this configuration the layout is always ready for instant operation, whereas the provision of lifting sections to span the entrance not only means that you have something to do before you can begin running, but it is also necessary to suspend operation should anyone want to enter or leave the railway room.

The terminus is fairly conventional, with the coal road facing in the opposite direction to the rest of the sidings. This road crosses over the main siding and has a further spur leading to an industry. A more elaborate industrial site is on the far side of the continuous run. These industries provide scope for specialized freight traffic and can excuse the introduction of more exotic types of wagon. For this reason we shall see further rail-linked industries as we progress. There is no need to specify the industry; one factory looks very

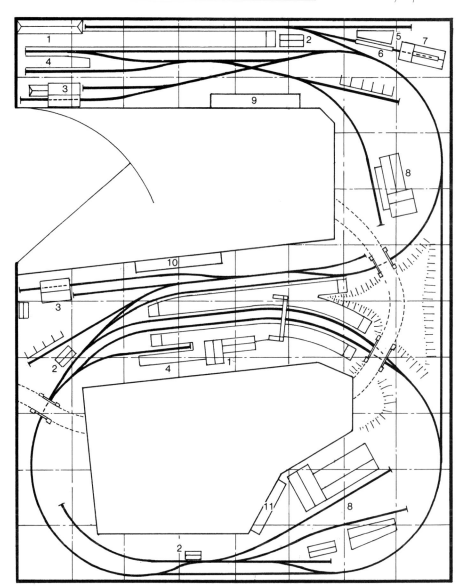

Plan 4 *Out and back system*
Key:
1 Station building; 2 Signal cabin; 3 Goods shed; 4 Cattle loading; 5 Coal stage; 6 Ashpit; 7 Locomotive shed with water tank; 8 Industry; 9 Main controls; 10 Junction controls; 11 Industry controls.

much like another and many old buildings have seen a number of different trades carried on under their roofs. Joe Bloggs and Sons Ltd can make anything from widgets to that

most useful of products, holes for washers.

Clearly, the further industry cannot be worked from the main operating well, and is reached by crawling under the baseboard. This is termed a duck-under, a sensible method of gaining access to operating wells, and when a third operator is to hand this line can be intensively worked.

There are a number of possible snags with this design. The locomotive depot tucked in the corner is reached by a kickback from the bay platform. However, as this is fairly long, there is room for three coaches to stand there without preventing access to the shed. The lack of a turntable is not serious, since we do have a triangle on which tender locomotives can be turned. There would be no difficulty in accommodating one if this was required. The previous plan shows how it could be arranged.

A more serious difficulty is lack of storage for stock and spare trains. One solution would be to replace the main industry with a series of loops and to hide these behind a low backscene about halfway across the further operating well. This would allow more space for scenic modelling, but would reduce the amount of visible track. It is a case of compromise between what we would like and what can be fitted into the space available.

Although it would be difficult to shunt the main industry from outside the further well, it does include a useful loop which would allow trains to pass one another on the continuous run, and it would be worthwhile arranging for control to be passed to the junction panel for this purpose. This necessitates a king switch to enable control to be transferred to whichever panel is required. At first

Although the North East is generally associated with coal mines and heavy industry, the old North Eastern Railway had a plethora of branches running through delightful scenery. Alan Wright set out to prove that the NER could give the GWR points and a beating when it came to creating a compact scenic model, as this corner of his 4 mm scale 'Cheviotdale' demonstrates. During the late '70s and early '80s this compact layout was a popular visitor to northern exhibitions, where Alan showed how one man could keep up a steady flow of trains during a whole day's intensive operation. Here a 'G' class 4-4-0 obstructs the level crossing while station duties are carried out.

Once upon a time it was said one should include a Southern Electric set on a layout 'to excuse the third rail'. Nowadays we see three-rail electrics running on battery power over two-rail systems. This 5BEL Pullman set, half of the sadly defunct Brighton Belle, *is running into the Newport Club's 'Long Suffren', which, being set in South Wales, is well off its beaten track. One of the minor pleasures in model railway operation is to include these impossible but attractive situations. Only the mean-minded would object.*

sight a multi-way changeover switch will do the trick, but switches that can transfer a number of circuits are not easily come by. A small bank of relays will do the job, with the added advantage that they can then be controlled from either panel. The circuit in Figure 16 shows how this is arranged. A

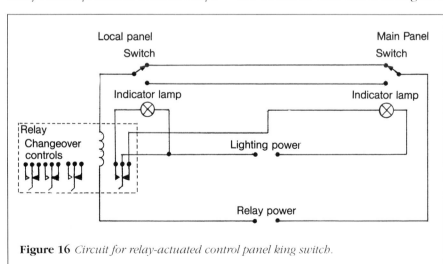

Figure 16 *Circuit for relay-actuated control panel king switch.*

pair of changeover switches is needed, and the wiring is identical to that used for controlling stairway lighting. As the switch position will not indicate which panel is active, indicator lights are needed.

In the USA, where large basements are common enough to allow designers to assume that modellers will have access to a large space, it is common practice to have all panels accessible from a single convoluted operating well. This is so convenient from every angle that fairly sharp radii are accepted so as to turn tracks back on each other along peninsular baseboards. Anyone interested in this approach cannot do better than to refer to the American-published magazine *Model Railroader* for examples of this approach to the hobby. Unfortunately, the practice of providing British homes with cellars ended about the time I was born (1924), but where a reasonably large space is available this

type of layout offers considerable scope for operation. In Plan 5 we have an extremely elaborate out and back scheme with no less than six stations, mostly double track and capable of handling quite large trains.

Starting at the terminus we have five platforms, two of which are relatively short and are mainly used by the local services. There is a large covered goods shed and a locomotive valeting depot. From here a section of quadruple track takes us to the outer suburban terminus, which also houses the main loco depot.

The line is now reduced to double track and swings round under a single track branch to a junction station. Here the branch curves away to climb over the main line and terminate at a small station on the other side of the doorway. The main line continues around the central peninsular baseboard and dives under the outer suburban through terminus to reach a four-plat-

Coal was once the staple traffic of British railways and a major source of revenue. In view of this a coal mine was once an obligatory part of any self-respecting model railway system, but the sheer size of the prototype became its downfall. Yet as this view of the colliery at 'Leasingthorne' shows, the atmosphere of a mine can be created in the corner of a layout. F. Warren's 4 mm scale model is based on North Eastern Railway practice in the Edwardian period.

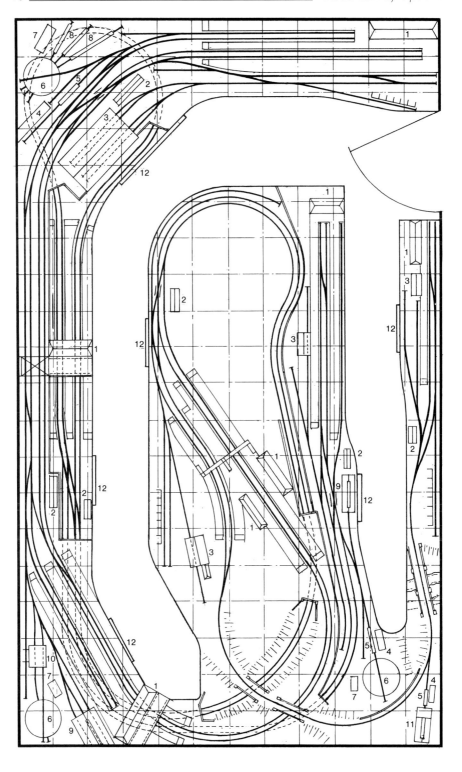

Plan 5 *Elaborate out and back system*
Key:
1 Station building; 2 Signal cabin; 3 Goods shed ; 4 Coal stage; 5 Ashpit; 6 Turntable; 7 Water Tank; 8 Inspection pit; 9 Locomotive shed; 10 Hopper coaling plant; 11 Locomotive shed with water tank; 12 Controls.

form through station, before looping around under the main terminus throat to return to the through station. A double junction allows the train to return to the main terminus or, alternatively, the line continues at low level to the secondary terminus adjacent to the doorway.

Six control panels are provided, but as they are all in a common operating well it is possible for one operator to run a service around the system. With diesel traction, using DMUs for the local and branch services, only sending a limited number of trains to the further terminus, a fairly complex timetable can be worked single-handed, but clearly with six operators a very intensive service can be run.

So far we have assumed that the controls are incorporated into the panel, which means the operator has a fixed viewpoint. The introduction of hand-held controllers has brought about the system of walk-around control, where only the point controls and section switches are located on fixed panels. In this system, the operator is the train driver and walks around the model, plugging his controller into convenient sockets. Some advanced electronic controllers do permit this to be done while the train is moving. Here the hand-held unit modulates the fixed control box. Alternatively, it is possible to have wire-free controls. The most favoured involve an infrared handset similar to the type used for TV and video control, though somewhat less complicated in use.

With walk-around control it is possible to take matters a good deal further and split the functions of signalman and driver by placing point and signal control under one or, more commonly, two central controllers who can pass control of a part of the model over to the drivers to permit shunting. In such systems, for larger sub-units such as loco depots and main goods yards, where movement can take place independently of the running roads, local panel control is normally provided, with provision for switching the entry/exit road over to the main panel for interchange.

This arrangement is very good indeed, providing certain pre-conditions can be met. First and foremost it is imperative to have a *disciplined* operating group. I will revert to this in Chapter 11. It is also essential to have at least two people in the group who are sufficiently interested in electrical matters to undertake the wiring *and maintain detailed records of the necessarily complex circuits involved.* It is also necessary to have somewhere to put the central panel where the controllers can see, in broad outline, what is going on. Ideally, it needs to be raised. Last, but by no means least, it is necessary to have a clear picture of the fundamental operating pattern, because the more involved the circuits you have, the more they dictate what can and cannot be carried out. In short, it only works well with an experienced, well-established group. However, it is so attractive from every angle that it makes good sense, at the initial stages of a large layout, to make provision for a centralized control panel so that in five, 10 or 20 years' time it can be built and installed, if that is your wish.

There is one feature of the centralized control panel that must be mentioned, namely cost. This is not merely the material used to build the panel, or the various switches involved; these are needed anyway. There probably will be additional indicator lights, but as they are good fun the cost is justified. What is easily overlooked is the fact that you are going to need a lot of wire, several kilometres in fact. What is more, a lot of the wiring will need to be put into trunking and, where it has to cross operating wells and access gangways, ideally carried under the floor.

CHAPTER 5
A matter of time

Any consideration of operation on a model railway naturally leads to thoughts of timetables, which brings us inexorably to the vexed question of time itself, and what appears to be an important subject: can you actually scale time? This topic emerges in correspondence columns at frequent intervals and leads to acrimonious debate. Matters are not helped by the fact that, within their self-imposed terms of reference, everyone is without any doubt whatsoever absolutely right.

We need to begin by realizing that we all juggle with time in the hobby. A steam age layout is a time machine, it takes us back into the past, and if it doesn't it is a failure. We also play fast and loose with time when we organize our operating sessions into model hours and model days. We talk of scale speed when discussing the performance of model locomotives and the operation of trains.

Any consideration of time makes one think of historical modelling, which is our excuse for including this view of Bob Harper's superb finescale 7 mm model of the imaginary GWR branch terminus 'Maristow'. A passenger train is about to depart behind a '517' class 0-4-2T, forerunner of the ubiquitous '14xx' tank. The train is in the familiar chocolate and cream livery, but the coach in the foreground is in the short-lived maroon livery of circa 1910. The locomotive to the right is a 'Metro' class 2-4-0T.

It is generally accepted that when the rpm of the model wheels match the rpm of the prototype, the model is travelling at the scale speed of the prototype. If the locomotive is either steam-powered or fitted with a synchronized sound generator, then the exhaust beats will sound right. From this we can show that scale time equals real time. But there is no need to get involved in tedious mathematics; this is self-evident because we have based our assumptions on one simple fact, that both model and prototype are being observed by one individual who is living in real time.

Let us consider another possibility, a fully detailed model of a church made exactly to scale, including not only a peal of bells but also a working model of the pendulum-driven tower clock. Not only would the bells sound tinny, but the hands of the clock would rotate at a rapid rate. Should anyone question this, there is a very simple practical test. Take a length of cord about a yard long, attach a small weight at one end and pin the other to the top of a door frame, thus producing a simple pendulum. Now make a model of this pendulum to your chosen scale. Set them both swinging and note the considerable difference in the frequency of swing.

This is not a wholly academic exercise, for it introduces the concept of meaningful scale time. When Froude began tank testing of ship models to predict the behaviour of the full-size hull before construction, he postulated Froude's Law which gives the conversion factor one must apply to dynamic calculations of model behaviour. I am not going to go into the boring mathematics since they have no application to our model world other than to explain why a model train travelling at a scale speed in excess of 100

A general view of Bob Harper's 'Maristow', showing the old baulk road, mainly associated with the broad gauge but still to be found on converted branches some 10 years after Brunel's magnificent if flawed experiment was finally swept away in a weekend in May 1992.

mph can happily negotiate a curve which on the prototype would initiate a derailment at anything above 10 mph. There are other points of difference between model and full-size dynamics, but fortunately the balance is normally in our favour. The main exception is the fact that the inertia of a model is extremely small and, accordingly, it is much more likely to bounce off the track.

There is an interesting historical misuse of Froude's Law. In the 1920s, Henry Greenly produced a number of tables giving, among other things, the supposed scale equivalents of weight. He also calculated the scale time using Froude's Law and discovered that in Gauge 1 a model day worked out at roughly two hours. Now it so happens that two hours is a reasonable time for an operating session and, furthermore, that if you reverse the drive to the hands of a clock, you also get a model day of two hours. He put two and two together and arrived at 22. It would be easy to deride this, but he is not the first and certainly will not be the last person to be deceived by a plausible coincidence.

We have now arrived at a different approach to scale time: the operating day or, to be more precise, the operating cycle. It begins with the various locomotives and coaches in a specific position on the layout and ends when they are all back in the same place. To a considerable degree, the same is true of wagons, but they are subject to slightly different rules that we will consider in Chapter 14. On a portable layout the model day should coincide with the normal running session. On a permanent system, where everything can be left where it is at any convenient point in the proceedings, the model day can easily stretch over half a dozen working sessions. To take an extreme case, Norman Eagles' 'Sherwood Section' needed the best part of an operating year to work through two model days.

The model day has to be shorter than the real day because inter-station distances are very much underscale, and therefore trains take very little time, real or model, to move from station to station. In addition, except at a very few extremely busy stations, there are considerable periods of near inactivity. There are many stations where the standard operating pattern is for there to be 15 minutes or so of frenzied activity followed by three-quarters of an hour of peace and quiet.

One way of dealing with this is to adopt a sequence timetable. Here, although the operating schedule is laid out as a timetable, the trains are run in sequence. In other words, when the 08:15 leaves, it is a quarter past eight on the model day. After less than 30 seconds of real time the 08:55 arrives, the locomotive runs round and departs, some 45 real seconds later, as the 09:12. This works well when there is only one station involved, and is equally effective when applied to a larger but essentially linear layout.

The alternative system is to use a speeded clock. I mentioned earlier that it used to be the practice to reverse the final drive on a clock, giving a 12:1 ratio. Inspection of a clock's mechanism will show that there is a distinct difference in the diameters of the holes in both hands, and the rearrangement is not quite as simple as it sounds. Unfortunately no published reference said how it was carried out and as everyone concerned is no longer with us, it is not possible to suggest how one should set about it.

Another approach is to remove several teeth from the detent wheel of the escapement. This is very effective with the traditional cheap clockwork alarm clock since not only are the gears very thin, but the extra kick generated by the faster speed also revitalizes a clock with worn bearings. The advent of the battery-operated quartz alarm and the mains-operated clock radio means that the traditional alarm is a dying breed, but there should be plenty of redundant timepieces on hand for some years to come.

The most satisfactory approach is undoubtedly the electrically driven speeded clock. This is made by removing the drive from an old-fashioned spring-driven clock and replacing it with an electric motor. This particular trick is best performed with a worn out cheap alarm clock, If one can't be found in the home, jumble sales usually contain at least one defective clock. Some form of drive is improvised, using some of the original gear train, with a 12 volt motor as motive power.

The clock is driven from a standard power unit, and provided with a vari-

able resistance to govern the speed and, most important of all, an on-off switch. If your sense of humour matches mine you can also include a reversing switch so that time can run backwards at will. The main point is that not only does the clock provide a point of reference for all operators, it also acts as a reminder of the position in the timetable reached at the end of the last operating session. Figure 17 shows the general idea. The details depend on the arrangement of the clock and motor in your possession, not to mention the extent of the scrap box.

Frequently a single large clock can be seen by all operators and serves as a common reference point. Nevertheless it would be pleasant were every panel to have its own clock, all giving the same reading. To the best of my knowledge this has never been done.

More 7 mm scale period modelling, featuring the Caledonian Railway and one of its most famous and best-loved locomotives, 4-4-0 Dunalastair, resplendent in the rich blue fully lined livery of the day. The scene is embellished by the characteristic station building. If one could seriously criticize this view it would be the poster hoarding on the left-hand gable end, advertising that encroaching English railway, the GWR.

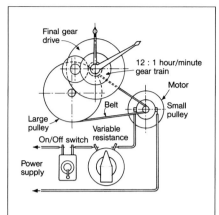

Figure 17 *Schematic diagram of electrically driven speeded clock.*

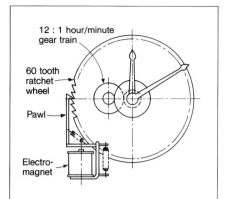

Figure 18 *Schematic diagram of slave clock driven by master pulse generator.*

One idea that has been put forward is to use digital readouts, which is certainly a good idea for any group with an electronic engineer in their midst. Unfortunately, standard quartz clock chips can't be used, as these are all set to real time. The demand for speeded clocks is nowhere near large enough to justify a custom chip.

An alternative is to use older technology, the electro-mechanical master/slave system shown in Figure 18. Here the minute hand is driven by a large ratchet wheel, actuated by a solenoid operated pawl. A 60-tooth wheel would be most convenient, as this would advance the hand in one-minute intervals, and the hour hand would follow though the standard 12:1 double reduction gear. The master pulse generator need be nothing more elaborate than a motor-driven cam operating a microswitch. This is a relatively simple model engineering approach, but it requires access to a lathe and an indexing device in order to produce a number of 60-tooth ratchets. There is also the business of building and assembling a number of clocks. Clearly, this can only be considered by a fair sized group who happen to have among them someone with the necessary skills, a well-equipped workshop and an interest in horology.

Having said that, this system has many advantages over the high-tech electronic approach. For a start, once built it is fairly robust, and moreover maintenance is well within the capabilities of any experienced railway modeller. We are dealing with mechanisms that are basically identical to those found elsewhere on the layout. Then the local clock has a traditional analogue display, and could be provided with a brass bezel similar in style to the railway pattern signal box clocks. It would harmonize with a set of miniature block instruments. A digital display only fits into a modern style push-button control panel.

CHAPTER 6
Evolving the timetable

The basic rule of the hobby is when in doubt follow the prototype. Although one can carry this a shade too far at times, it is a fairly safe bet that full-size practice provides an excellent guide for the model. When we consider the operation of the model and timetables in particular, we realize that there is no inherent reason why we should not follow the same rules and procedures in our miniature world as are observed on the real system. As always, we must follow them at a respectful distance, since apart from all else we do not have anything like the resources of a full-size railway system.

The main problem, whether we are working in 1:200 or 1:1 scale, is creating the initial timetable. There are few

Modelling a steam age prototype branch line station has its problems, not the least of which is that if sufficient information is available to build the model, it includes awkward details such as the working timetable and, above all, the normal make-up of trains that worked the service. This model of 'Kingsbridge', terminus of the former GWR branch from Brent Junction in south Devon, is a faithful copy of the prototype, but the trains are anything but typical. The branch was normally worked by the smaller '45xx' 2-6-2 tanks hauling one or two B sets of non-corridor stock, about the only thing not visible in this photograph. However, shuttling the same set of coaches and the same locomotive back and forth does get a little boring, and does not make for an interesting display at an exhibition. Modeller's licence is a wonderful thing.

things more daunting than staring at a blank sheet of paper, wondering where to begin. It is easier on the prototype since there are customers to tell you what they would like; passengers demanding trains at a specific time, manufacturers and merchants requiring a freight service. We can only simulate this on the model by creating an imaginary community, and from this getting some idea of the sort of service required.

First, for a British or European model, we need to sketch in the essential passenger service. With a USA-based system, freight is the mainstay, and in many areas there is no more than one passenger service a day.

There are three main strands in passenger services, long-distance travel, short trips to nearby towns, and daily commuter services. Although the latter are mainly associated with large conurbations, even the quiet country branch had its regular travellers. There were no extra trains involved, though an additional strengthening coach might be provided. The important point is to have a service laid on at the appropriate times.

Long-distance services need to be geared towards two separate types of travel. Business travel requires one very early train to the main city, generally London, with a return working leaving sometime between 5 and 6 pm and getting back sometime before 11 pm if possible. This would probably involve two round trips by a single

rake of coaches, providing a pleasure and family visit service, which while not particularly profitable in itself, takes advantage of the need to utilize the stock, train crews and track capacity.

There would also be some local traffic in the middle of the day, with a small morning peak when cheap day returns became available. Much of this will be pleasure and shopping trips, but in rural areas there will also be a small amount of essential midday and evening travel for such things as visits to hospitals.

We can now start to construct a basic timetable for a model branch line. Although our model only consists of a terminus running to a fiddle yard, we need to consider the whole network, which is shown in Figure 19. The figures alongside the lines are the timings of a normal service. Although I have given the model a set of fictional names, with the obvious exception of London, the resemblance to the former Seaton (Devon) branch will be noted. There is, however, one important difference. We are assuming that there is an Ayville–Easburg through service by some trains, so that we can have a greater variety of working over the branch. As I said before, we should follow the prototype at a respectful distance.

We are catering for two types of commuter traffic, manual workers who begin work at 8 am, and office and professional staff who start at 9. We are assuming that Easburg has a range

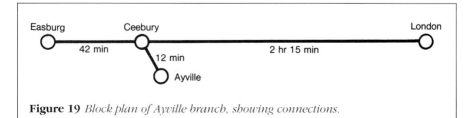

Figure 19 *Block plan of Ayville branch, showing connections.*

of engineering and manufacturing companies, while Ceebury has a milk depot, which also produces cheese, cream and butter, together with a small factory dealing mainly with agricultural equipment. Most of the office work is in Easburg.

Allowing a two-minute stop at Ceebury, the journey by through train A to Easburg takes 45 minutes. This might seem to offer the possibility of a trip every hour, but the need to change engines, allow the crew some time not only to attend to the needs of the locomotive, but also to their personal requirements, means that a 70–75 minute interval is more reasonable. Again, train B can't quite make a round trip in half an hour, for although with push-pull working the driver has only to change ends, the guard has not only to attend to the parcels traffic, but also to test brakes and make entries into his log. In theory he could do this while travelling between stations, but it is a good idea to have the entries in legible handwriting.

Apart from this, there are the passengers to consider. The experienced commuter, burdened only by one piece of hand luggage and a newspaper, can and will get in and out rapidly. An elderly passenger, carrying three shopping bags and decidedly weary at the end of a heavy day, will move more slowly, even if in good health. A family with three children ranging from 18 months to five years, with a

pushchair to fold, will take even longer to get inside. Anyone at all ill or disabled will also need to take their time. Of course, we must not forget the occasional railway enthusiast. He may be very agile at getting on and off the train, but has first to run to the front end to photograph the locomotive and note down its number, shed code and, if time permits, find out the names of the crew. As somebody once remarked, we could run a perfect railway if it weren't for the passengers. Therefore reasonable connections should be scheduled at Ceebury; we can assume three minutes from Ayville to Ceebury and five minutes in the other direction.

Bearing all this in mind we can start working out our schedule and in Timetable 1 we have a workable preliminary schedule for the early morning trains. We could go on to complete the day, but we now need to consider other factors.

First, there are the London trains, four of which are shown in Timetable 2. These trains will normally omit local stops and therefore are scheduled to cover the Ceebury–Easburg section in 25 minutes. Here the main consideration is the departure time from Easburg in the up direction and London in the down. We are assuming that they all observe the same pattern of stops and running times. This is reasonable if we also agree that the main express service between London and Easburg

Timetable 1 *Basic service on Ayville Branch, early morning*

		B	A	B	A	A
	B					
Ayville	*dep* 06:20	07:33	07:46	08:25	:	09:48
Ceebury	*arr* 06:32	07:45	07:56	08:37	:	10:00
Easburg	*arr* 07:17	:	08:30	*09:12*	:	10:34

		B	B		B		
	B						
Easburg	*dep* :	*07:26*	:	:	08:43	:
Ceebury	*dep* 06:48	08:03	:	09:01	09:17	:
Ayville	*arr* 07:00	08:15	:	09:13	09:29	:

Timetable 2 *London–Easburg trains connecting with Ayville*

Easburg	│	06:35	07:35	↑	19:47	21:47
Ceebury	│	07:02	08:02	│	19:20	21:20
London	↓	09:22	10:22	│	17:00	19:00

doesn't provide a connection between Easburg and Ayville. This now gives us the schedule timings at Ceebury. The express will only make a one-minute stop here, so the branch service must be there in good time. In addition, if the connection from Easburg is made by the through service A, it must wait until the express has left, and the two-minute stop we allowed could be extended to 15 minutes or more.

These timings will have an effect on connections as the 07:35 from Easburg calls at Ceebury four minutes behind the provisional timings of the local train. At some stage these two trains will meet, so we move the local train two minutes earlier and loop it at Ceebury. From this we now have Timetable 3, which adds the London timings; our businessmen from Ayville are going to have a while to wait at the junction for the first train. What happened at Seaton once ownership of cars became a significant factor was that anyone wanting to go to London simply drove into Axminster, or took the bus and made a better connection. However, in a model world such things don't happen.

It will be seen that there are no arrivals from London in this part of the table, and the express from Easburg does not have a scheduled connection to Ayville.

Before we go on to consider the rest of the service, there is the little matter of the branch goods train. On most relatively short branches this was worked by the branch locomotive. On most model railways it provides an excuse for using another locomotive, and so we only need to find a suitable path between the passenger trains. In this situation, there would be one morning goods train, collecting the wagons that were loaded on the previous day and leaving a fresh supply of loaded vehicles. A path exists along the branch at 07:05 from Ceebury, arriving at Ayville some 17 minutes later.

We'll leave the middle of the day until later, and look at our returning commuters. Although in the morning there is an hour between the starting

Timetable 3 *Ayville Branch timetable, early morning*

		B	B	A	B	A	A
Ayville	*dep* 06:20	07:33	07:46	08:25	:	09:48
Ceebury	*arr* 06:32	07:45	07:56	08:37	:	10:00
Easburg	*arr* 07:17	:	08:30	*09:12*	:	10:34
Ceebury	*dep* 07:02	:	*08:02*	:	:	:
London	*arr* 09:22	:	*10:22*	:	:	:

		B	B		B		
London	*dep* :	:	:	:	:	:
Ceebury	*arr* :	:	:	:	:	:
Easburg	*dep* :	07:24	:	:	08:43	:
Ceebury	*dep* 06:48	08:03	:	09:01	09:17	:
Ayville	*arr* 07:00	08:15	:	09:13	09:29	:

A prototype set on a busy main line offers more scope for running an interesting mix of trains. Bill Oake's 'Berkhamstead' offers, if anything, too much choice since one would need a massive set of storage sidings to be able to reproduce the LMS timetable with absolute authenticity. However, one can run typical expresses headed by large locomotives, such as this anonymous Royal Scot *4-6-0.*

times of manual and white collar workers, they finish work at the same time. At most there is a variation of half an hour between companies. This brings us to the consideration of the local services along the main line, which will connect with the branch shuttle.

We also need to consider through services from and to London. If we

Still at 'Berkhamstead', we now have a down goods running through on the slow lines behind an LNWR Cauliflower 0-6-0 goods.

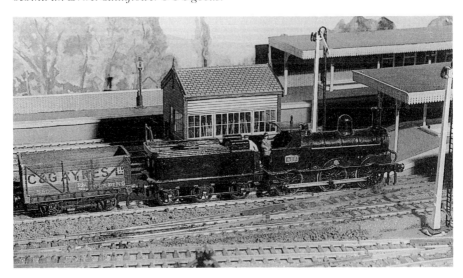

Above *LNER 'G5' 0-4-4T No. 1769 backing on to its train at 'Dawarton'. The leading van conveys small parcels.*

Below *A small branch sub-shed, showing the coal stage with a light hand-operated crane for lifting the filled buckets of coal up to the bunker. The water tank can just be seen on the extreme left. The LMS '4F' is an unusual visitor to the shed at 'Dawarton'.*

Above *GWR 0-6-0ST heads a freight train through Coldrennick Road Junction on Bob Harper's 7 mm scale layout.*

Below *A short local train in the spur platform at 'Benfieldside'. The rear vehicle is a horse-box, a very common addition to local trains up until the mid-1950s. Note the varied load in the wagons at the rear.*

Above *Shunting in progress at 'Piel Quay'. This 3/16 in scale model is based on Furness railway practice, but was being jointly operated by members of the S Gauge Society at IMREX, hence the mixture of companies.*

Below *A short local runs on to the pier station at 'Port Sandford', a fictitious South Coast ferry terminal. The GWR condensing pannier on the left has wandered a long way from its normal haunts, the Metropolitan line to Smithfield and the environs of Paddington.*

Above *Watching the trains go by over an impressive viaduct on the Yeovil MRG's 4 mm scale 'South Junction' layout.*

Below *An early 1980s scene on the Croydon MRC's 4 mm scale Southern Region exhibition layout. A coal train enters the station while a Scottish Region push-pull set stands at the platform.*

Above *GWR 'Bulldog' class 4-4-0 hauls a set of four-wheeled coaches past an LMS goods on the Ilford & West Essex MRC's O gauge layout.*

Below *GWR '14xx' 0-4-2T on freight duties on the Macclesfield MRC's 4 mm scale 'Botley Town'.*

Above *Turntable and locomotive valeting facilities can be neatly tucked into a corner.*

Below *A Southern electric set hurries through the countryside, a sight far more common in full size than it is on the model.*

Above *Push-pull, North Eastern style. Fletcher 0-4-4T BTP sandwiched between a pair of adapted non-corridor coaches, seen on F. Warren's 'Leasingthorne'.*

Below *Wagon loading in action. The 4 mm scale loading plant on Geraint Hughes' Cromford & High Peak model can deliver fine limestone chippings into the waiting wagons.*

Above *A freight train rumbles over the viaduct on the MRC's 2 mm scale 'Chiltern Green'.*

Below *Gretley Colliery on Norman Eagles' 7 mm scale 'Sherwood'.*

decide that these are adequately provided by a through coach, we can stable it overnight without too much trouble. If Ayville is important enough to warrant a daily through train, then we have two choices: a train that returns to London as soon as possible, or one that is stabled overnight.

A train leaving London at 10:00 would arrive at Ayville at 12:40, allowing 15 minutes for reversal at Ceebury. In the steam age the London train would have been headed by a tender locomotive, facing towards Easburg. Even with the 15 minutes allowance for reversal, there isn't time to turn the loco, so the more likely arrangement would be to use the locomotive from train B to haul the coaches up and down the branch. This is not what we want on our model, so we stretch probabilities and bring the train down with the main locomotive, *travelling tender first*. This is explained by the simple fact that there is a turntable at Ayville but not at Ceebury. While the locomotive is being turned and watered and its ashpan cleared, the porter at Ayville goes through the coaches tidying up. Quite apart from the need to give the local passengers a reasonably clean train, he will collect most of the day's newspapers and, on a good day, several magazines as well. The toilet header tanks will also need refilling.

Allow 40 minutes for this. The train would then depart at 13:20, arriving at 16:00. However, while the through train is blocking the main platform loop, we cannot also accept the other loco-hauled passenger train A during this time, though Train B can shuttle in and out of the bay platform.

I have not prepared a complete timetable for this hypothetical case. Instead, I suggest that you produce one yourself as an exercise, either using the parameters I have given, or amending them to suit yourself. While doing so, remember that you need to consider the capacity of the model station since you cannot hold more stock than you have tracks for it to stand upon. It is a good idea, in the preliminary planning stage, to rough out a timetable to ensure that you do provide sufficient platform space and siding accommodation.

In full-size practice, service plans are frequently drawn up in isolation before being passed to the timetable office to establish whether either the stock or the paths exist. If they don't, unwanted changes are forced, mainly against the best interests of the passengers.

On the model it is much more fun to test the new timetable out in the flesh, making notes of any problems as you go along. Once any discrepancies have been discovered, the timetable is finalized and serious operation can begin. One important point to remember: at the end of a cycle, usually 24 hours, but in some cases one week, all locomotives and coaches should be back in their original position so that the routine can begin again.

When I spoke of the goods train I mentioned a spare path. As the main object of a timetable is to ensure that two trains do not try to occupy the same space simultaneously, it is necessary to ensure that they have a clear route throughout. This is a little difficult to visualize in the abstract, but very easy to see on a train graph. On this, distance is plotted vertically and time horizontally, while a track diagram is placed vertically along the distance axis as in Figure 20. This shows the main running tracks and storage sidings, which have an important bearing on the operation of the model. The graph is more readily drawn on squared paper, though if a drawing board and T-square are available, it is possible to set out the base lines with this.

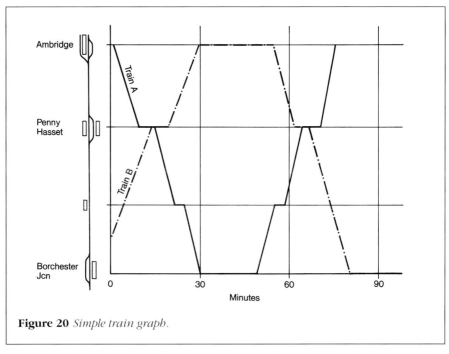

Figure 20 *Simple train graph.*

We can now draw in the paths of the trains on this diagram. For the purposes of our illustration, the lines are of different weight and style: in practice coloured pens can be used. Prototype train graphs are printed for the purpose, so that graphs can be quickly prepared. It is possible to use a photocopier to produce a limited number of copies, though if large numbers are required, this could prove costly. Some savings can be made if two or three of the long, relatively shallow graphs are drawn on a single A3 sheet of paper and, after photocopying, cut on a guillotine. A much simpler method is to mount the graph on stiff card, cover it with transparent plastic and then use chinagraph pencils to prepare the diagrams. These lines can be quickly rubbed out with a dampened cloth.

The slope of the line is an indication of the average speed of the train. The nearer the vertical, the faster the train. A horizontal line indicates that the train has stopped. Up and down trains are indicated by the handing of the slope. As the line is single track, the lines must cross at the passing loop. This is all fairly obvious from the diagram.

Although the train graph provides a very accurate picture of the overall situation on the line, it is not true to suggest it is a clear picture; there are too many closely spaced lines for this. Prototype train graphs are very large affairs indeed, anything upward from a metre in length, and are frequently kept rolled.

The main disadvantage of the train graph for the modeller is that it needs to be produced on a large flat working surface. Working out timings with pencil and paper only needs a firm A4 pad, pencil and rubber. This is where the continental pattern, wide pitch, squared paper really comes into its own, since you can easily align the columns, even when balancing the pad on your knee in a well-filled commuter train. Such paper is available from better stationers. Timetable compilation, to the extent we need go, can be carried out well away from the layout in one's spare moments.

It is always possible to base your own timetable on a prototype schedule. While the public timetable only lists passenger trains, all train movements are listed in the working timetable (WTT). At one time these informative documents were supposedly for official use only and, unless one knew a friendly railwayman, unobtainable. In recent years out-of-date WTTs have been sold to enthusiasts. More important, most modern detailed line histories include a number of WTT extracts depicting the development of services over the years.

Of course, if the model is closely based on an actual prototype, the prototype WTT should be followed. The only snag with this is that the popular single track branch usually had a very boring service; often the same push-pull train shuttled up and down the line all day. One way round this difficulty is to have two timetables, one authentic but dull, the other imaginative but exciting.

Although we have so far only considered a relatively simple layout, based on branch line practice, the same procedures can be applied to more complex layouts. Naturally, the main line schedules would be worked out at the start, any branches being dependent upon the core timings. As a large layout does not spring into being overnight, the timetable can develop with the system. There is no need to

The Keighley 7 mm Group chose to model an imaginary prototype in 'Ravensbeck', taking care to ensure that all details were taken from actual North Eastern Railway prototypes. As a result they were able to tailor the operating schedule to the stock available and to the storage capacity of the loops. The line was accordingly worked to a timetable that allowed any viewer who was prepared to stand long enough at the lineside to see a realistic sequence of authentic Edwardian trains running past. Many fascinated visitors spent as long as an hour soaking in the atmosphere as a result.

stress the importance of starting serious operation at a fairly early stage. Most of us are only too keen to see something running. It is, I think, essential to introduce timetable working the moment sufficient track is laid and in working order to permit this, certainly well before the scenic work is begun. Working to a timetable can reveal deficiencies in the layout plan, and it is best these are found before changes involve too much scrapping of one's work. Into the bargain, in the early stages the timetable is going to be much more straightforward.

Every established timetable, whether model or prototype, is the product of a good deal of fine tuning or, if you prefer, to be blunt, trial and error. It is rare that a timetable is completely recast, though sections do get revised when a section of line is extensively modified, or there is a large-scale change of motive power. Even so, the new schedules retain traces of the old. In particular popular trains remain at or about their traditional timings to retain public goodwill. Generally, the trend is towards simplification, with regular interval services operating throughout the day with a fixed pattern of stops.

While model timetables are similar to prototype schedules, there are important differences. In full size the purpose is to show an operating profit, or at the worst to keep losses to a minimum; on a model the object is to have fun. Attaching and detaching through coaches or routing through trains is much more interesting than arranging connections between independent trains. Remarshalling rakes of coaches and coupling and uncoupling train engines is far more engaging than shuttling a fixed rake backwards and forwards, whether it is an InterCity express or a humble Pacer.

On a model railway space is always at a premium, and there is rarely room for one to spread out a complete timetable beside the control panel. In addition, it is not that easy to read a timetable directly whilst in the middle of running a train, whether model or prototype. On the full-size railway, signal box registers and individual train schedules are used. For the model the flip card has been devised to provide the operator with a simple, easily assimilated digest of the timetable.

Flip cards are written or typed on

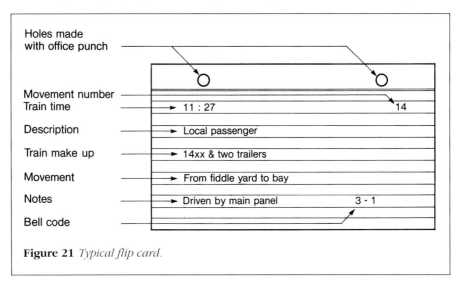

Figure 21 *Typical flip card.*

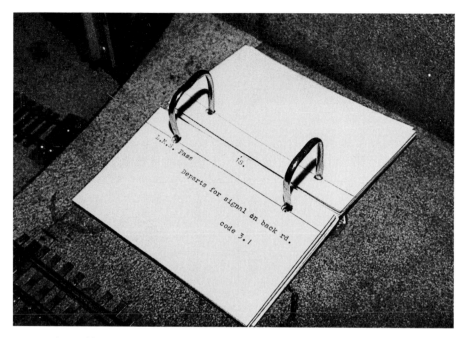

A typical set of flip cards in action. The uppermost card shows it is move 18, an LMS passenger train, which will leave the fiddle yard on the left to wait at the signal on the back road before proceeding. The bell code, 3 pause 1, is also given.

to standard small office filing cards, and provide the necessary information to allow the operator to identify the next train movement. A typical card is shown in Figure 21. The information is, in order, the movement number, train time, train description, train make-up, the movement covered together with notes and the bell code (if one is being used). The amount of detail included is a matter for individual choice. One can add the section switches to be thrown, the arrangement of points and the signal lever to pull. These details are obvious to the experienced operator, but they are invaluable to a knowledgeable visitor.

The flip cards have a pair of holes, at the standard 80 mm centres, punched in the top. They then fit neatly on to any twin-ring clip. As the cases of arch files and ring binders usually wear out before the inner mechanisms, it is usually possible to

acquire these fittings for no more outlay than the effort of drilling out the rivets holding them in place. The holes so provided take wood or metal screws to provide a firm fixing to the control panel.

In use, the operator turns the card over at the end of each movement, hence the name. Generally, the experienced worker peeks at the next couple of cards during lulls and prepares himself for the following moves. The movement number is critical, since it is used to co-ordinate moves between the various operators.

One obvious question to be asked is, 'Can one use a home computer to generate a timetable?' A lot depends on the computer, for the current price of powerful PCs brings impressive computing power within the reach of the private individual. A great deal more depends on the availability of suitable software programs, but as the

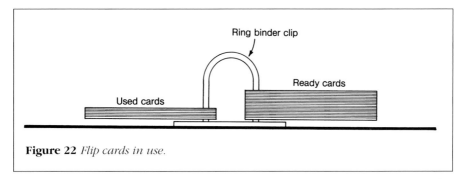

Figure 22 *Flip cards in use.*

sort of programs used by full-size railways have to be specially written and take over a year to compile, it would appear that simple pencil and paper methods must rule the day.

However, inside information from London Transport timetable offices suggests that the main function of the computer is not to generate the timetable, but to eliminate the drudgery of filling in and keeping track of the details. At the same time, it materially reduces the time between the finalizing of a new schedule and the production of a printed timetable for the operating staff. This points the way to a simple application of computers to our needs.

On a model railway, the most tedious part of timetable production is preparing the final neat draft. Frequently this means that only one timetable is prepared, and there is a great reluctance to alter it. This is where even a simple home computer can be called into play, for even the most elementary wordprocessor allows one to prepare a tabular printout with relative ease. However, a spreadsheet is probably easier to use for table production, even though most of its features would not be employed.

A database is best for the production of flip cards. The train movement will need to be the key field, and should be alphanumeric so that extra moves can be inserted (eg, 11a). To get a correct sort, you will need to enter 01, 02, 03 etc for the initial nine numbers (001, 002... 010, 011... if you need more than 99 movements). The label print option would allow the data to be produced on self-adhesive labels which are then applied to the cards.

As data can usually be transferred from one package to another, even if an integrated suite is not available, one can have the best of all worlds. But I warn you, it isn't easy or automatic, because although the facilities are there the instructions and tutorials, unsurprisingly, make no mention of this rather specialized, off-beat use of a computer.

The great advantage is that once the master file has been entered, checked and safely backed up on a spare disc or tape, the table can be amended, while an additional table can be readily printed out. What if it takes a little time? The machine can be set up and then left to get on with the job while you're eating a meal, watching TV or, best of all, operating the layout.

CHAPTER 7
Fiddle yards

Trainspotting is mostly a matter of standing at a suitable vantage point with an ABC list in one hand, a ballpoint pen in the other, ready to underscore the number of every locomotive you see. There is another variant: standing at a vantage point with a timetable in your hand, watching the trains go past, knowing where they have come from and where they are going to. The fact that you can only see them on a small, insignificant frac-tion of their journey is immaterial; you follow the whole journey in your imagination.

You can do this on a model railway by just modelling one station, ideally one where there is plenty of action, and this method of operation has a couple of obvious advantages. It reduces the demands on space, and at the same time makes it a simple matter for one enthusiast to build and operate a thoroughly satisfying model

A typical sector plate fiddle yard. Note the relatively high sides, which add strength and protect the stock, and the several locomotive spurs provided to the right. Spare goods stock is stored on the sector plate for swapping. A modified domestic bolt is used to align the roads. The tracks are spaced widely to allow for easy handling of the stock.

single-handed within a reasonable timescale. Again, imagination provides the rest of the train movement, though some physical provision has to be made for the model train to complete its run. In essence, we take our lead from the theatre, where actors enter or leave the set according to the needs of the plot and, when off-stage, can collect fresh props, change their costume or even amend their make-up to help create the illusion.

The off-stage portion of the layout is provided by the fiddle yard. No one individual invented this feature, and I can't even recall who first applied the term to something that has been variously described as hidden storage sidings, reversing sidings and magazine sidings. I did encourage its use since, as will be seen, it is descriptive of its function and most common method of use in Britain.

The idea arose when it was realized that if you provided some hidden storage loops somewhere along the line, not only could you store complete trains out of sight, you could also alter their sequence on the visible section of the layout. This was particularly important when implementing the out-and-back scheme where a terminus was complemented by a reversing loop, since without the provision of several spare tracks on the hidden section, your trains operated a boomerang service — every time you sent one out, it came straight back at you. The same idea was applied to through stations, where a series of loops was provided on the far side of the oval. We will be dealing with storage loops in more detail in the next chapter.

In this section we will concentrate on the true fiddle yard. This comprises a set of parallel roads that, by one means or another, can be connected to the main line of the layout. It holds enough complete trains to permit a varied operating pattern to be fol-

lowed. In one sense it has no real existence. In another it is the rest of the railway system. Because of its imaginary status, there is no need to have anything more than plain track. Furthermore it is not necessary to follow prototype methods of marshalling and reforming trains. Initially, it was thought of as a means of complementing a modelled terminus when there was insufficient space for a reversing loop, but very soon its potential for timetable working was appreciated, and the terminus-fiddle yard arrangement became a dominant theme in British railway modelling. It is

Looking along a five-road train turntable on Jim Hewlett's 'Blaen-y-Cwm'. A removable Perspex stop is provided at the far end, the marks on this showing clearly how often a train has hit it during operation. The stop for the other end can be seen on the left. The photograph also shows how the need to align the ends of the tracks increases the width of the table.

also applied to through stations, particularly in an exhibition context.

Initially, fiddle yards began with a fan of turnouts and ended with a turntable as shown in Figure 23. In this way it was possible to run a train in, detach the locomotive, turn it and, after running round the train, reattach it. It was later realized that if you just lifted the locomotive off and put it down at the other end, you could save a lot of bother. For obvious reasons, this is known as a crane shunt.

The next step was to eliminate the points by using some form of swivelling or sliding base, saving not merely the cost of the points but also reducing the overall length of the fiddle yard into the bargain. The swivel base or

sector plate is the most common type today, and a typical arrangement is shown in Figure 24. The sector plate forms a trough, with the far end blanked off to prevent trains diving over the end on to the floor.

A small refinement is provided by fanning out several short radial tracks (Figure 25) from the sector plate, so that spare locomotives can be held on these lines. With this arrangement it is not always necessary to pick up the locomotive to reverse the train. It is also possible to provide for alignment with other exit tracks, and this can produce some interesting arrangements in the station, either by providing a means of getting a locomotive back on shed, or allowing a goods train to be

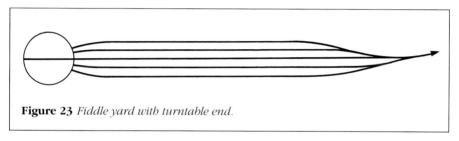

Figure 23 *Fiddle yard with turntable end.*

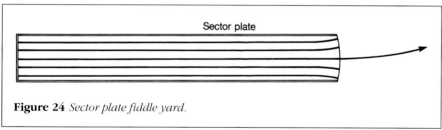

Figure 24 *Sector plate fiddle yard.*

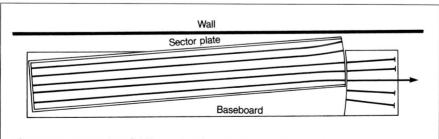

Figure 25 *Sector plate fiddle yard with radial locomotive roads.*

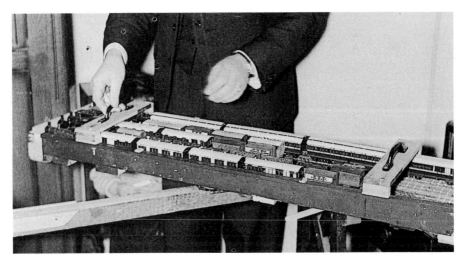

Peter Denny turning his first train turntable on the old portable 'Buckingham'. In this version the five-track table lifted off and formed the stock storage when the line was dismantled, hence the wooden bridges with stout metal handles. The five roads are parallel and set at standard double track centres since the stock does not need to be touched.

backed into the imaginary goods yard. This diagram shows the main snag with the sector plate. When used against a wall, as is usual in the home, the sideways movement is restricted. This in turn restricts the number of tracks that can be fitted. Generally speaking, five is the maximum, but it is possible to accommodate eight where there is little or no restriction on the swing.

An obvious extension of the sector plate is the train turntable shown in Figure 26. Here the whole train can be turned around. Clearly this requires a good deal of room and often can only

be used when the layout is shown at an exhibition. In the home it may only be possible to use it as a sector plate. With the train turntable, the end stops need to be moveable, and a popular method is to provide a U-shaped stop that swings up out of the way. Another important feature is the need to provide a good, free-running pivot. One possible source for a free-running bearing is the hub of a bicycle wheel. This has a good pair of ball-bearings that can take side thrust when on the bike and, in this case, will take care of the vertical load instead.

The snag with both the sector plate

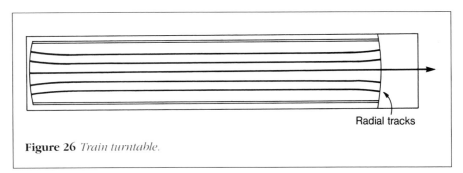

Radial tracks

Figure 26 *Train turntable.*

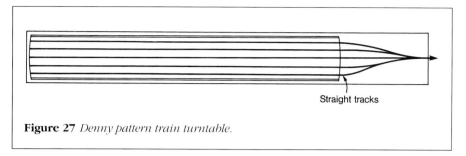

Figure 27 *Denny pattern train turntable.*

and the train turntable is that it is extremely difficult to arrange for remote control. It can be done, but it is definitely a skilled job to make the mechanism. Not only is it necessary to construct a fairly powerful but slow-moving, smooth drive to the unit, it is also essential to provide a method of indexing the table so that it aligns exactly with the entry/exit track, and then to provide a positive locking mechanism which also energizes the appropriate track.

Peter Denny looked at this problem and applied some fine lateral thinking. A fan of points can be remotely controlled with readily available commercial point motors. If these then feed all tracks of a train turntable, it is merely a matter of arranging the timetable so that it is only necessary to turn the main storage section end from end once in the sequence. Obviously, this solution, shown in Figure 27, does require a good deal of space, but given that, the entire set-up, apart from the reversal of the table, can be automated.

A locking mechanism is a necessity rather than a refinement on both sector plates and train turntables. This not only ensures alignment of the tracks, but can also be a means of energizing the correct track. The most favoured system is to fit a bolt to the side of the approach road, and then to have a series of sockets on the sector plate. Figure 28 shows how this is done. A cheap and equally effective bolt is fab-ricated from brass plates and brass or copper tube as shown in the diagram. It is essential to have the bolt a good sliding fit in the tube, so you may well have to buy a couple of feet of suitable diameter rod in order to get the necessary few inches. Alternatively, several standard aluminium domestic bolts can be used, one of which is used as supplied, and the rest cannibalized to provide additional sockets. In either case, electrical supply to the track can be completed through the bolt so that nothing can move on the sector plate until the table is locked. The return rails are bonded together, and connection between the sector plate and the rest of the layout must be by means of a length of flexible wire. With train turntables flexible wires are out of the question, so it is necessary to employ contacts. Figure 28 also shows a simple means of preventing stock sliding off with a train turntable. A piece of ply is dropped between two sets of vertical slides.

An alternative to the sector plate is the traverser. This is slightly easier to make as all roads are parallel, and feeds to the tracks can also be taken through flexible leads. Smooth sideways movement is most readily produced by using a set of plastic drawer guides, available from any DIY store if you cannot salvage some from disused furniture. Even better are the ball-bearing slides used in office filing cabinets, providing you can find a battered and broken cabinet and have the

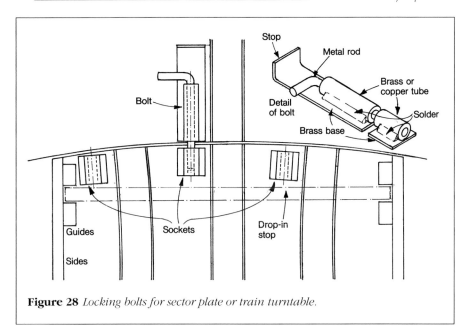

Figure 28 *Locking bolts for sector plate or train turntable.*

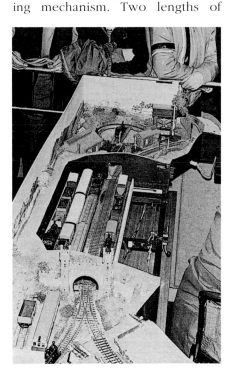

tools and tenacity to dissect it. Figure 29 shows a large traverser in plan, and sketches in a fairly elaborate operating mechanism. Two lengths of screwed rod, obviously identical, engage in nuts under the table. The rods are coupled by bevel gears and a long length of plain rod, and a further bevel gear drive to a handle completes the arrangement. A word of warning: this is not a set-up that can be botched. Proper bearings, firmly supported, must be provided for the rods if it is to work at all. Providing the table is not too long, a pair of drawer handles is extremely effective.

It is a little unrealistic to send a rake of wagons out of a terminus, only to have exactly the same rake return on the next freight working, but the fiddle yard allows us to get round this problem. The wagons are removed and a fresh set, taken from stock, put in their place. At the same time, any loose

The five-track traverser fiddle yard on Alan Wright's 'Cheviotdale'. It will be seen how much space is needed behind the table to allow the tracks to align with the main circuit. This leaves a good deal of space in the corners which has been ingeniously utilized for a locomotive depot and further stock storage.

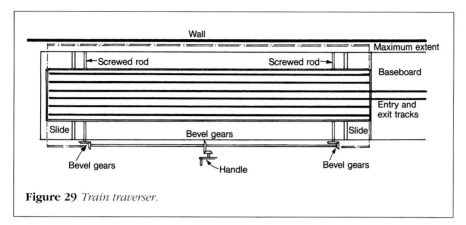

Figure 29 *Train traverser.*

loads are removed and replaced. In a similar fashion, through coaches and other vehicles added to passenger trains can be swapped around. Clearly, one needs to provide suitable storage for these vehicles, and one solution, very popular at exhibition venues, is to fit one or two high-level shelves to the screen provided to shield

the fiddle yard from public view. This is shown in cross-section in Figure 30. The shelves are provided with rails on which to stand the stock. While standard track can be used, two lengths of strip wood can be pinned and glued to form a rough track. If a saw bench is available, a pair of grooves can be cut in the timber instead.

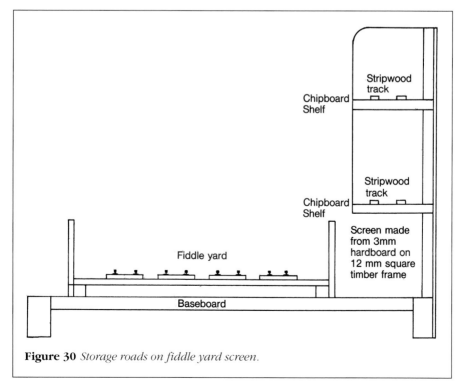

Figure 30 *Storage roads on fiddle yard screen.*

There is another recent approach, particularly popular among finescale modellers who find it is undesirable to handle locomotives or rolling stock to any extent, and this is the train cassette. Mechanically, it is ridiculously simple as can be seen in Figure 31. Two lengths of aluminium angle, at least 25 mm square, are secured to a length of wood with the inner edges set precisely to gauge. At each end there is a standardized fitment that mates with a housing at the end of the entry/exit track, and this not only aligns the angles with the track, but it also makes all necessary electrical contacts. Each train is provided with a cassette. It is picked up, turned around and replaced when required, the train remaining undisturbed throughout. A separate cassette is normally provided for the locomotive. So far all such systems use a standard length cassette, although longer trains can be run by coupling two train cassettes together. The system is completed by a transit box designed to take several cassettes. The main blemish in this scheme is that cassette length is limited, and anything over four bogie coaches in 4 mm scale is too long for easy handling. It is also very labour intensive in use, and is not conducive to rapid turnround. Given that train lengths are severely limited, I feel that a train turntable is preferable on many counts.

Whilst fiddle yards are traditionally associated with termini, they may be used to operate a through station. Figure 32 shows the principle in block form, and indicates how easy it is in a small space to have more fiddle yard than visible layout. Needless to say, this is not a good idea. This type of layout is growing in popularity among exhibition operators, since the main snag — the length needed — is of less importance in the exhibition hall. It requires a minimum of three operators, if anything like a worthwhile service is to be maintained.

Perhaps the most valuable feature

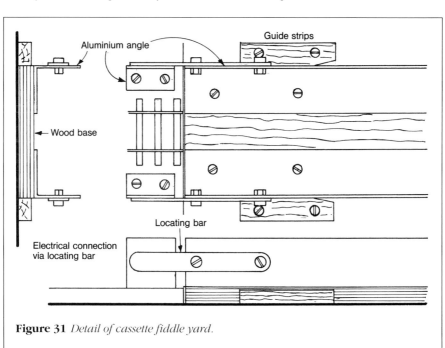

Figure 31 *Detail of cassette fiddle yard.*

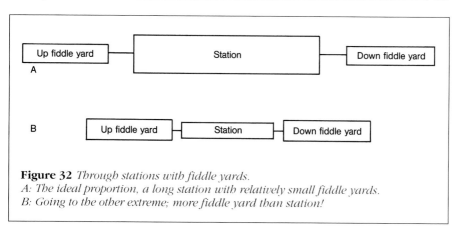

Figure 32 *Through stations with fiddle yards.*
A: The ideal proportion, a long station with relatively small fiddle yards.
B: Going to the other extreme; more fiddle yard than station!

of the fiddle yard is that it does increase the capacity of the layout enormously. Five or six tracks can be fitted into the space needed for a terminus that could only hold two full trains at any one time. It is not the perfect solution — two or three series of loops arranged to double back offers even greater scope, but this requires an extremely large space, even in N gauge. For most railway modellers, some form of fiddle yard is the best way to increase line capacity and help create the illusion of reality.

CHAPTER 8

Watching the trains go by

Full-size railway operation intersperses long bouts of steady running with occasional short bursts of frenzied action at stations. Not surprisingly, most beginners consider that it is a good idea to have a fair stretch of unencumbered main line on which to see trains in motion. Few would argue with this, but the difficulty lies in the fact that unless it is properly done, it can soon get very boring.

This can be easily demonstrated with a basic train set. A plain oval of track only allows us to run the train around in circles. It is always possible to mount this simple circuit on a baseboard and embellish it with bits and bobs of scenery, but as long as you have the same train going over the same circuit time and time again you have a sterile situation. This is exacerbated by the confined nature of the layout.

Often the first thought is to increase the operating interest by providing additional tracks, or by twisting the track into a convoluted spiral. This produces a more interesting scenic picture but fails to address the root of the problem. It's really quite obvious. What we are attempting to do is to put the viewer in the position of a trainspotter, standing at a strategic viewpoint alongside the track, *watching the trains go by*. What we have to do is to provide some means of having more than one train on the circuit.

This is where the second common

error occurs: an attempt is made to introduce more trains on to a simple circuit. There are two distinct ways of allowing two or more trains to run independently on a single section of track, automatic and command control. It is often claimed that they provide the answer. Automatic control is extremely complicated to design and install. Command control, where any individual locomotive may be controlled independently by means of a superimposed carrier control signal, is relatively simple to install, if one overlooks the business of fitting the modules into smaller locomotives. It is, however, extremely expensive. These inherent faults would be tolerable if they addressed the problem; unfortunately they do not.

Let's go back to our trainspotter. During his sojourn at the lineside he will observe a series of different trains passing his vantage point. He will take notes and possibly photographs to record what he has seen. He does not expect to see a succession of identical trains passing by; indeed he would be extremely astonished if this happened. Yet this is what we will get with the plain continuous circuit, no matter how long it is and how many trains we can squeeze on to it.

The provision of some hidden storage, no matter how elementary, transforms the situation. The layout is now divided into two distinct sections, the 'real' portion, which should be fully developed scenically, and the 'off-stage' portion that is just plain track on bare baseboard. Plan 6 shows how this can be done on a relatively small lay-out.

The visible station depicts a simple steam age passing station on a single track branch, with just sufficient siding space to allow reasonable freight operation. We have a two-track yard with a goods shed and a couple of coal bins on one side, and a single siding serving the cattle loading on the other. This spur also finishes in an end loading dock so that wheeled vehicles can be easily run on and off flat wagons. Before the turn of the century, this was an important if occasional traffic, as long-distance road travel was regarded as uneconomic.

The passing loop is incomplete. Double track runs round to the storage sidings, which provide two tracks for each direction of travel, one of which is technically reversible. Despite the fact that it only appears to provide for two trains in each direction, with a little ingenuity we can arrange for three trains. There will be two main passenger trains, with a basic three-coach formation with the option of adding a passenger rated van. One of these will almost certainly be hauled by a tender locomotive — a 4-4-0 or 2-6-0 would be in keeping. The other will be headed by a 2-6-2 or 2-6-4 tank. A third passenger train will be a two-coach push-pull formation, which can easily shuttle back and forth in either direction. The fact that the same train goes in either direction only adds to the authenticity, since it is a local shuttle service.

The final train is a pick-up goods train, possibly headed by an 0-6-0 tender loco of suitably antique appearance. This will need to be re-formed off-stage to provide a proper varied freight service, using spare wagons which stand on the empty areas of the

Plan 6 *Single track passing station with hidden loops.*
Key:
1 Station building; 2 Signal cabin; 3 Goods shed; 4 Cattle loading.

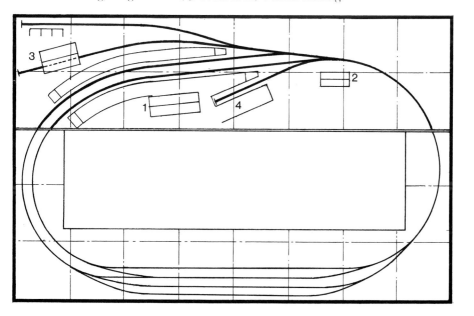

hidden section. Taking matters a stage further, the main passenger trains could also be reversed, creating the illusion to the viewer that they had gone to their destination and then returned. This will be emphasized if the two main trains have an obviously different make-up, whilst that addition or removal of trailing vans will add to the illusion. A viewer standing outside the layout will see a slice from a cross-country branch operation.

In my opinion, the single track passing station is best suited for a small layout, since the dramatic effect is raised by the need to pass trains in the loop. Whilst this is a steam age model, the fact that many former double track lines have been singled make this basic design suitable for diesel era modelling, but alas, the goods yard would have to go. It can be replaced by a company siding serving an industry. For authenticity, the physical remains should be modelled: the cattle loading bay would be full of rampant weeds, the goods yard would be a car park, and the goods shed turned over to commercial use. The station building might even be replaced by a modern bus-stop glass and steel structure.

This layout is particularly suited to exhibition use. It is essentially theatrical in its approach: we have the stage, the scenically developed 'real' section and the wings and dressing rooms, the storage or staging loops. The trains are the actors: they come on to the stage, play their part and make their exit. We now have the option of pageant or drama. In the former case the trains merely emerge from one side, pass in front of the audience and then disappear. In the drama mode, having emerged into the 'real world' they perform some sort of action other than simply running through and pausing at the platforms. Clearly, both elements tend to merge into each other. For example, on a single track line the trains pass each other.

For that matter, Plan 7 is also exhi-

LMS streamlined 'Pacific' City of Lancaster in original livery heads a train of maroon coaches through Bill Oakes's 4 mm scale model of 'Berkhamstead'. The S.C. Pritchard private owner wagons in the foreground are authentic and have no connection with the well-known manufacturer.

bition-oriented. Unlike all other plans, it is drawn out for N gauge — 4 mm scale would require an enormous space. With ample length, the hidden loops are arranged in tandem, giving six tracks on each of the main lines and a further loop for the branch. The plan follows that of Seaton Junction as I knew it in the 1950s and '60s. Unfortunately, I did not take note of the actual track arrangements at the time, and no reference book in my collection provides a plan of the final arrangements. The track formation shown does allow the prototype train movements to be duplicated, and the buildings can be correctly located. It ought to be possible to produce a model that looks close enough to the original to satisfy most people.

The scheme is particularly suited for exhibition, where the operators would stand behind the model, facing the storage roads, whilst the visitors would stand in front, watching the trains go by. The branch shuttle service will add extra interest, even if it only runs in and out of the bay. However, the working of the prototype was a little more complicated than that.

The basic operating pattern was straightforward. The centre roads were normally used by trains not booked to stop, but on occasions they were occupied by freight trains waiting to allow a passenger train to get ahead. There was very little local goods traffic, but the milk factory made up train loads of milk tankers bound for Vauxhall. The Seaton branch was worked by a shuttle train. A daily through coach was brought up the branch and shunt-

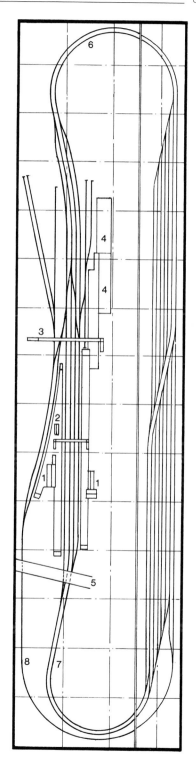

Plan 7 *Four-track station based on Seaton Junction.*
Key:
1 Station building; 2 Signal cabin; 3 Footbridge; 4 Milk factory; 5 Main road; 6 To Honiton and Exeter; 7 To Axminster and London; 8 To Seaton.

ed over all four roads to be attached to the rear of a three-coach local for Templecombe. There it was hooked on to the rear of an express. The return working had the coach attached to the ACE (Atlantic Coast Express) as far as Salisbury, where it formed the last coach of a local train to Exeter. After stopping at the platform, the train would move forward until well clear of the junction, whereupon the branch train would back on and collect the coach before proceeding down the branch without pause at the platform.

In the 1950s the last train from Waterloo, the 18:00 down express, did not stop at the junction. Instead the Seaton push-pull would run empty to Axminster on Friday and Saturday nights to collect the occasional passenger. I deliberately use the singular; more than once, I was that passenger. It was inevitable that the train was axed and the local bus took over. Now even the bus service has gone.

Crossovers are shown in the storage roads to allow this movement to be duplicated.

The long footbridge was provided to preserve an ancient right of way across the railway. It was still there when last I saw the remains of the station, traversing a large empty space.

Even in N gauge such a layout requires a good deal of space, so in Plan 8 we look at an alternative approach in a moderately large room, working in 4 mm scale. The looped eight formation is used to provide a longer run, but there is only room for a straightforward single track through station. The platforms are set out on a generous curve to save a little space, and there is a small goods yard, but this is essentially a layout where one watches trains go round in circles. Loops hidden behind a low backscene allow one to vary the sequence.

This is at variance with the usual arrangement of layouts of this nature,

Plan 8 *Looped eight double track station.*
Key:
1 Station building; 2 Signal cabin; 3 Goods shed; 4 Cattle loading; 5 Controls.

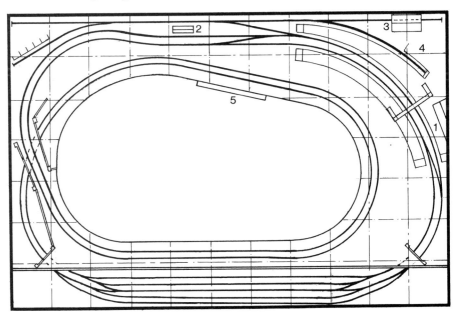

The archetypal GWR branch train, a '14xx' 0-4-2T and auto-trailer, drift lazily along the branch on Ken Payne's 4 mm scale layout.

where the loops are located under the station. Whilst this has its advantages, the disadvantages are considerable. Of these the difficulty of access is paramount. It is not merely that it would be necessary to build the station on readily removable sections, but also that the gradients would need to be much steeper to provide the extra clearance needed for this. Not only would the framing for the station sub-bases need to be taken into account, but the need to reach under to extract a derailed vehicle would also mean that extra clearance between the underside of the board and the tracks would have to be provided. With the present arrangement, a difference of only 70 mm is needed at the crossing point, whereas 150 mm would be barely adequate for under station loops.

This is only one consideration. Trains held in under baseboard loops cannot be seen, and in order to prevent one sending a fresh train into an occupied loop elaborate detection circuits are needed. Even so, the operator would only know a loop is occupied,

not what sort of train was standing on any specific road.

Although it would appear that the situation in the open loops would not be obvious to the operator, the addition of a pair of wing mirrors would enable him to see the situation at a glance. It might be advisable to add a couple of small spotlights to ensure that the stored trains were not in shadow; this is something that can be determined by experience.

I have only shown five loops, the centre one being arranged for reversible running. Seven would be better and I think could be arranged within the space indicated, but when producing a project plan to a scale of 1:16 it is best to err on the side of safety. Anyone inspired by this proposal should spend a good deal of time setting out the loops full size, using point templates in order to cram in as much storage as possible. With this type of railway, the storage loops are the essential feature and should be given most attention, another reason I think it best not to hide them under scenery. The station is purely cosmetic. Were I building this type of layout I would omit it and substitute a viaduct. But then my main reason for making such a line would be to automate it.

Watching trains run past is very relaxing. With a fully automated tailchaser, all one needs do is to settle oneself down comfortably, throw the main switch and then watch the pageant pass before you. I have dealt in some detail with basic automation in my book *Model Railway Wiring* (published by Patrick Stephens Ltd in 1989), but some general comments are needed. A limited amount of work can be done with simple bi-stable relays, but ideally the sequence should be driven by a control unit. At this point computers spring to mind, and anyone well versed in the intricacies of interfaces and programming could do worse than build the whole thing around a second-hand computer. The obsolescent 8-bit machines are fully up to the job. The Acorn BBC, which is very robust and comes with an interface port as standard, would be a good choice at the time of writing. You certainly don't need a state of the art machine, nor do you need anything more advanced than tape storage, since the essence of railway operation, whether model or full-size, is a linear progression.

However, the main snag with using computers to control model railways lies in the fact that they are much better suited to simulation. There are programs around that allow one to 'drive' trains over actual routes, or to take the part of a signalman in a centralized signal box. The latest developments in multimedia work, with CD roms providing massive amounts of storage, open the possibility of near virtual reality on a desktop.

More basic control schemes can work well and are easier to design and understand. The heart of the system is the program machine, which can take

two forms. One is a paper loop which is advanced step by step as the timetable proceeds. Punched holes in the tape allow various contacts to be made to energize points, start trains and so on. Alternatively, the selection can be made by a Strowger multi-selector switch. This useful device, once the heart of an automatic telephone exchange, is capable of controlling a predetermined sequence of events. As it can still be obtained, it is probably the most suitable for the experimenter, who will more than likely end up with a bank of relays looking rather like an old electro-mechanical telephone exchange. Clearly this will only appeal to those of us who positively enjoy this side of the hobby, but it is worth thinking about when designing the layout.

Although double track lines appear to be the most suited for continuous running, a single track model provides more action, since the need to pass trains means that positive action needs to be taken to alter the points and start and stop the trains. Such a scheme is shown in Plan 9, which is inspired by Alan Wright's 'Cheviotdale', but occupies a more generous area. As a result the station is much more ambitious and represents a station on a cross-country branch serving a large market town. This is the reason for the very extensive, albeit cut-down, facilities provided. In addition to the goods yard we have a rail-connected industry, a small locomotive depot and a long lie-by siding which can hold a complete train. The crossover in the centre of the long loop is there so that not only can a goods train be shuffled across the station and into (or out of) the lie-by siding, but it is also possible to run round a train without having to be in possession of both single line tablets.

Instead of loops, we have a six-track traverser. This saves a good deal of length, but requires a good deal of

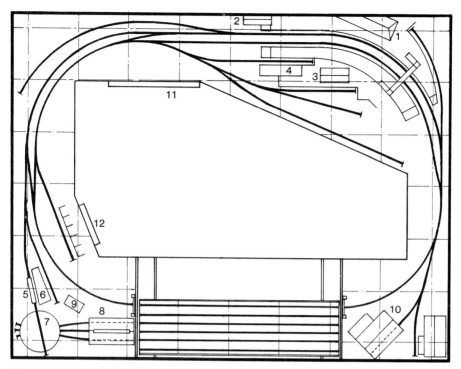

Plan 9 *Single track passing station and traverser.*
Key:
1 Station building; 2 Signal cabin; 3 Goods shed; 4 Cattle loading; 5 Ashpit; 6 Coal stage; 7 Turntable; 8 Locomotive shed; 9 Water Tank; 10 Industry; 11 Main controls; 12 Locomotive depot controls.

width; this is emphasized by showing the table in its extreme position. As always, one has to balance advantages and disadvantages and then exploit the result. In this case we have what could be a good deal of wasted space in two corners. Instead we are able to utilize the two bottom corners more effectively. The small industry needs little comment. As usual I haven't specified anything, but bearing in mind the size of the town a gasworks would be very appropriate. The other corner contains the locomotive depot.

This is a fairly large sub-shed, with a three-road engine shed which apparently holds that many locomotives. Look carefully and you will see that the shed roads coincide with three traverser tracks and, as the shed backs up to the backscene, you've probably guessed that these roads connect, allowing some subtle swaps to be carried out. It is possible to introduce extra loco storage roads at the front, and these could be hidden under large industrial buildings, with removable panels so that there would be no obstruction during running sessions. With these extra holding tracks, it will be quite a simple matter to reverse trains on the traverser.

Two control panels are provided, but I only envisage one operator. The second panel controls the locomotive depot and also has any switches needed to isolate tracks on the traverser. The one operator would simply turn round to deal with locomotive movements.

Although in general one can operate a loco depot from a distance, since coupling and uncoupling is not involved, here we have a small diameter turntable which must assume any one of eight positions. Whilst commercial turntables which provide even more index positions are readily available — at a price — they are large diameter affairs. This table is only large enough to take a 4-4-0 at a pinch.

The construction of an indexed turntable is not an easy task and I wouldn't blame anyone for going to any length to avoid the chore. Equally, I'd not advise trying to modify an N gauge turntable, as this is even more fraught with difficulties. On the other hand, the simple manually operated table using a straightforward worm drive from a handle on the baseboard edge is a project well within any model maker's capacity. Its only disadvantage is that it has to be operated by someone who can see what he is doing.

It might be helpful to have a further panel by the industry. This need only

Plan 10 *Junction with dumbbell and linked branches.*
Key:
1 Station building; 2 Signal cabin; 3 Goods shed; 4 Cattle loading; 5 Waiting rooms; 6 Ashpit; 7 Coal stage; 8 Turntable; 9 Locomotive shed; 10 Water Tank; 11 Industry; 12 Access hatch; 13 Main control; 14 Branch controls; 15 Locomotive depot controls; 16 Industry controls.

control the points and include any section switches, since with this type of layout train control is most conveniently arranged with a hand-held unit. The traverser is small enough to be moved by hand. Indeed the layout is eminently suited to the modeller who prefers to keep the controls simple.

One objection to this type of layout is that the provision of a continuous run encourages tailchasing, where the same train is left to circle the tracks endlessly. However, this objection is not so much to the design of the layout, but to the method of operation. It should never be forgotten that there are times when there are good reasons for allowing a train to make several

Ex-North Staffordshire 'L' class 0-6-2T heads a local train of Midland non-corridor compartment stock at 'Blidworth' on Norman Eagles' 7 mm scale 'Sherwood' section.

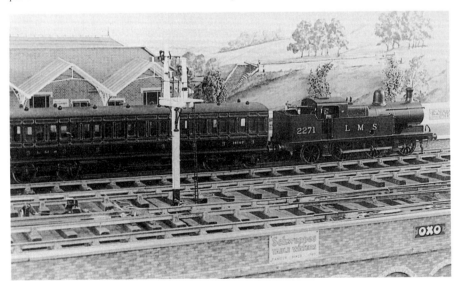

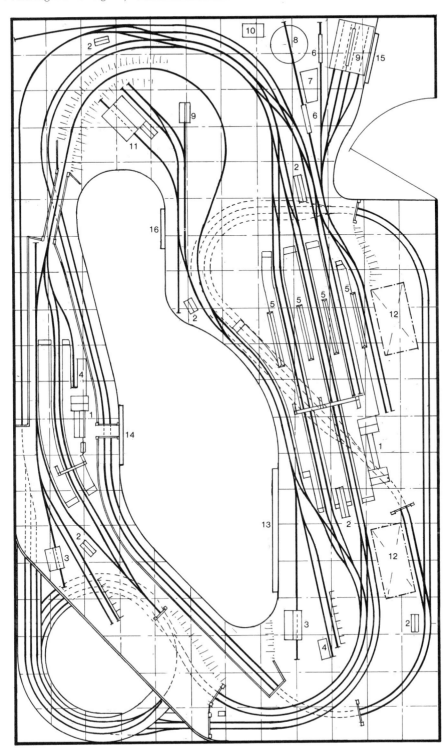

laps of the continuous circuit. A more serious objection is that even when one does arrange a sequence, after a time the same train reappears travelling in the same direction. In reality, it should return from the opposite direction.

There is a track formation that creates this illusion — the dumbbell. This can be looked at in two ways, either a pair of reversing loops on either side of a station or an elongated oval continuous run which has been pinched in the middle until the two sides form a section of double track. Its only disadvantage is that it takes up a good deal of space.

Plan 10 shows this to the full. It occupies a very large room, actually an attic room in a house I once owned. This is why the door is in a rather awkward position. We have just the only large junction station laid out in a generous fashion. There are four main platforms, leading on to a section of quadruple track which diverges as it enters a tunnel and reaches one set of storage loops. At the other end of the station the double track main line runs completely around the room, mostly in full view until it divides to form a loop under the main station. I'd prefer not to do this myself, but the doorway prevented me from putting it in the opposite corner.

There are two branches which snake around to meet in a common set of storage loops. An earlier draft included reverse loops on both lines, but result-

ed in a horrendous series of interlaced lines and the virtual obliteration of the visible main line. The branch station has a third loop, primarily for goods traffic, but this can be used to terminate trains if one wishes. This and the loco depot have independent panels, but these are mainly for the benefit of visiting friends. I envisage this layout being owned and operated by one enthusiast.

It represents what I think is the most one individual should attempt on his own, and moreover is only the third draft; the idea would stand a good deal of refinement. There is, for example, a very long duck-under to get to the operating well. The only way one can get access to the junction at the top of the plan is to remove the industry, which needs to be on a separate baseboard. Indeed, I am only showing a principle, though I've no doubt many people would find it an exciting concept.

As for that matter I did when I first learned of Jim Savage's 'Tone Vale'. This plan is an attempt to cram part of his concept into rather less than a quarter the space he has been able to give to his magnificent model of the old Great Western around Taunton. This is not merely the ultimate in operating realism — it is run on a timetable based on the mid-1930s' GWR WTT — it is also a magnificent place to watch trains go by just as they did when we were young.

CHAPTER 9
Branch line operation

The branch line prototype has, for the past 40 years, enjoyed considerable popularity. Originally put forward as a solution to the extreme post-war housing and model shortage, it has now established itself as part of the mainstream of the hobby in Britain. The classic branch line model is based on a terminus serving a small town of around 5,000 inhabitants. It is often claimed that this permits true-scale modelling of actual stations in a moderate-size railway room. This is not strictly true since most branch line stations sprawled over large areas of land which, when purchased, lay on the outskirts of the town. It was not merely a matter of low cost. There were no existing buildings to limit the size of the station, which was often laid out on a lavish scale to allow for an increase in traffic that rarely materialized.

The classic model branch prototype is the short feeder line. Passenger train lengths were short, frequently just one or two coaches, allowing one to reduce the platform length savagely and still run scale-length passenger trains. As most of the direct observation of branch line working took place in the 1950s and 1960s, when road had taken away much of the freight, the fact that a goods train in the line's heyday often exceeded 20 wagons can be conveniently overlooked. Feeder branch stations usually had a simple track plan. This allows the overall size of the model to be reduced by 50 per cent or more without altering the design or, with two provisos, the method of working.

The main point to watch is the kick-back siding, exemplified by Ashburton, terminus of the Great Western Railway's branch from Totnes which

E.T.D. Revill's 4 mm scale branch terminus based on Ashburton. This high-level shot shows that the overall length has been considerably reduced without destroying the character of the original. However, it is clear that in order to shunt the mill siding to the bottom left, the entire goods shed would have to be clear.

is shown in Figure 33. Here the mill siding was taken from the single goods road. On the prototype there was sufficient clearance between the mill siding turnout and the end of the rake of wagons to allow a locomotive and one or two wagons to sneak in. Even so, this meant so much juggling that more often than not the wagons were hauled into the siding by means of a length of rope hitched to the drawhook of the locomotive on the main line. This had to be released before it fouled a telegraph pole and constituted an illegal fly shunt. But as was remarked on more than one occasion, Ashburton is a long way from Paddington and what the top brass didn't see needn't worry them.

Another method of getting wagons to these awkwardly placed sidings was for the van to be dropped at the most convenient point and then hauled to the loading point by the station's horse. Horses were used for rail cartage well into the 1950s because they could double up as shunters, something a motor vehicle cannot do.

It will also be seen that although Ashburton had many interesting features it lacked a signal box, being worked on the single engine in steam principle between the passing station,

Buckfastleigh and the terminus. This method of operation only allows one locomotive to operate over the line at any one time. At Ashburton this was interpreted loosely; providing one locomotive was on the shed road, another could be brought in. As I said, it was a long way from Paddington.

Single engine in steam was a very useful principle on the prototype, and is even more useful on the model. Not only does it allow one to omit signals, but it also means that there is no need for elaborate electrical arrangements. Only one controller is needed, preferably hand-held, and any isolating switches are usually confined to the fiddle yard. Beginners please take note.

Not only is it possible to copy the exact track layout of a branch line station, the addition of a fiddle yard allows one to copy the actual working timetable of the branch. In the early days of the model branch boom it was by no means easy to lay one's hands on a working timetable, and so the more common practice was to add a freight service to the published passenger timetable and fudge the picture slightly. However, in the intervening years many detailed histories of branches have been published which

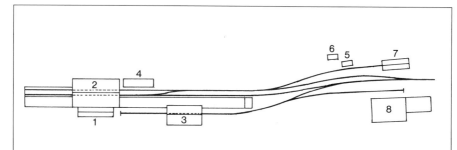

Figure 33 *Ashburton station, GWR.*
Key:
1 Station building; 2 Timber overall ('Brunel') roof; 3 Goods shed; 4 Cattle loading;
5 Coal stage; 6 Water tank; 7 Locomotive shed; 8 Industry (mill).

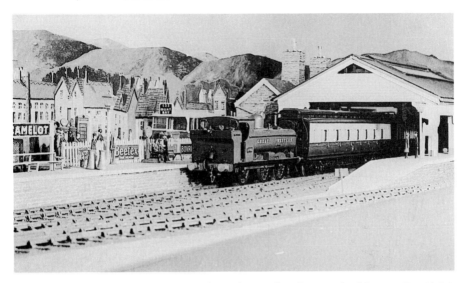

You can't get away from Ashburton! The timber roof and station building on David Salisbury's 7 mm scale station 'Camelot' are near accurate models of the popular prototype. An important difference is the absence of side panels on the train shed, which not only makes it possible to include an additional platform, but also provides a decent view of the station building.

include reproductions of the actual working timetables.

Unfortunately a careful study of feeder branch WTTs shows that the operating pattern was, not surprisingly, also very simple. The branch train shuttled back and forth to the junction several times a day. The main variation was that on the shorter branches something approaching a rapid regular interval service was set up, whereas on longer lines some attempt was made to get the trains to connect with the main line service. This was not always done as well as it might have been, another reason the branches gradually lost traffic through the 1950s, and why this chapter uses the past tense.

A few branches have survived into the diesel era, but often they are little more than long spurs over which a railcar set shuttles back and forth. As a stand-alone model they offer no operating interest whatever. There are, however, a few surviving branches which exist mainly to serve an industry. Frequently there is no passenger service at all and invariably there is just one type of traffic, generally a bulky mineral which is more conveniently moved by rail.

To return to the steam age, branches normally had an engine allocated to them, and quite a few had a single road shed at the terminus to house it overnight. This was invariably a sub-shed of a nearby motive power depot, and at regular intervals the branch locomotive would be exchanged so that routine maintenance could be carried out.

For most of this century the locomotive was auto-fitted so that it could work the one, two or three coaches allocated to the service as a push-pull train. This eliminated the bother of running round at the terminus and the junction, where all too often there was no convenient run-round loop and, in a few cases, no provision for the branch train at all.

There were two basic types of push-pull train, with mechanical or air-operated control gear. The mechanical pattern was used by the Great Western Railway, and had a shaft running under each coach, ending in a universal joint that could be coupled to the next coach or the engine, where it could be linked to the regulator. This limited the number of coaches that could be coupled to either end of the locomotive to two, and so with a three- or four-coach formation, the locomotive would be in the middle. Apart from the regulator, the driver had control of the brakes and could operate the locomotive whistle by means of a pull cord. As a result, the second man had to be a passed fireman, an experienced railwayman who was deemed fit to drive a locomotive, but was waiting for a vacancy.

The Southern, LMS and LNER preferred air-operated gear, a trifle more complicated than the simple mechanical linkage. This placed no limit on the number of coaches that could be coupled to the locomotive. Although this theoretically would have allowed steam-worked commuter trains to be push-pull operated, the Ministry of Transport frowned upon the practice, though it was common on the Continent. Diverging from the branch theme, the modern InterCity trains with driving trailers are the ultimate extension of this principle.

Steam railcars had a brief flourish around the turn of the century, and in the guise of the Sentinel steam railcar survived until the 1940s on the LNER. The railcar's main weakness was inflexibility. Few were capable of hauling more than a van as tail load, whereas the loco-hauled push-pull could not only haul extra coaches and suitable goods stock as well, but the loco could also be detached for other duties, principally working the branch freight. Diesel railcars were introduced on branches in the late 1950s, but the earlier GWR railcars were originally used for lightly loaded cross-country and outer suburban duties. Modeller's licence has allowed them on to feeder branches.

Few branches had more than one goods train working a day. Ideally this ran early in the morning so that the necessary shunting could be finished before the local traders came into the yard to collect and deliver. Frequently the branch locomotive worked this service as well. For a beginner, a train service that only requires one locomotive, two or three coaches and around 15 to 20 wagons has a considerable appeal.

However, at this level, branch line operation can soon become very boring. In particular, push-pull working is very dull. There is no need for the locomotive to run round its train, so apart from the daily goods working there is no station working involved. This is fine when the branch is an offshoot of a larger system, but less than satisfactory when the branch terminus is the layout.

The solution is to introduce through services. This is justifiable since many branches did enjoy this luxury. Typically it was no more than a through coach, normally a brake composite coach, an all-in-one vehicle designed for this purpose. Indeed, up to the early part of the century, when the then second class was phased out, there were tri-composite coaches. When bogie vehicles came into general use in the 1890s, some magnificent vehicles were built specially for through traffic between most reasonable and many improbable pairs of towns. Many of these vehicles survived until the end of the Second World War. Branches serving seaside resorts usually had a through train or trains on summer Saturdays. Very occasionally there might be a regular service to a nearby large city.

A more satisfactory arrangement for a model branch service is to postulate a route long enough to require two train sets to sustain an hourly service, enabling one to have a push-pull (or diesel railcar) as well as a loco-hauled set. Add to this a regular through working and haul the daily goods with a separate locomotive, throw in the occasional special train, and you get a more varied pattern.

The question now arises, where do you put all these trains? On the prototype they would end up somewhere along the main line. We have chosen to model the branch terminus precisely because we did not have room for the main line in the first place. This is where the fiddle yard comes into play as shown in Chapter 7.

Let's look at this in some detail with examples. Plan 11 is the archetypal L-shaped terminus-fiddle yard branch, arranged on four rectangular baseboards plus a sector plate fiddle yard. For storage the pairs of station baseboards can be fixed face to face, using end spacers, turning them into a simple crate.

The units are fairly short, which keeps the overall weight of a pair down to manageable proportions, and also makes it possible to pack the layout into the back of a small hatchback. It is arguable that if the layout won't fit into the family car, it isn't portable. The small size of the units also makes storage in the home much less fraught. Fiddle yards are long units that do not fit readily into small cars, but they can go on a roof rack.

Before we look at the operation of the station, a word about the control. This is effected from a separate control panel, which is linked to the layout by means of flexible multi-core cables and multi-pin plugs and sockets. Rather than take a mass of wires into one baseboard unit and then have multi-pin jumpers, individual feeders are taken to each of the three main boards. The two further sections, which do not need many connections, are linked by jumper cables. With this arrangement the location of the control panel can be changed, which can be invaluable when the line goes to an exhibition.

The station layout is conventional. The platform has a run-round loop and bay road. There are three sidings in

Plan 11 *L-shaped feeder branch terminus.*
Key:
1 Station building; 2 Signal cabin; 3 Goods shed; 4 Cattle loading; 5 Coal stage; 6 Ashpit; 7 Loco shed with water tank; 8 Turntable; 9 Industry; 10 Sector plate fiddle yard; 11 Controls; 12 Multi-pin connectors; 13 Jumper cables.

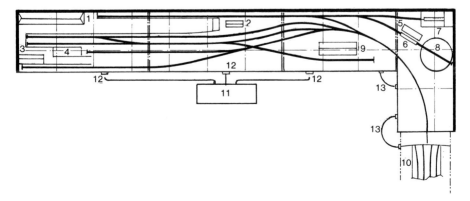

the yard, and a further track leads off the run-round loop, over a diamond junction to a rail-connected industry. This avoids the problems of the kick-back siding, discussed earlier in this chapter.

The loco depot is reached from the bay road, but as there is ample room between the entry point and the plat-form, this is not at all inconvenient. The coal stage and ashpit are located immediately in front of the turntable, for the shed road would be unused for most of the working day. Indeed it would only be needed when there were two locomotives in the station at once. The turntable would be used to turn tender locomotives, which nor-mally travel with the locomotive at the front. Older readers will recall that Meccano Ltd considered this so uni-versal a rule that they did not fit work-ing couplings at the front of their Hornby Dublo express passenger loco-motive models.

We have been dealing with steam age branches, but a few remain in the diesel era. In some cases the branch is no more than a long spur road, end-ing at a platform all but devoid of facil-ities. In others the branch, while closed to passengers, remains open to serve a local industry, usually a quarry. Plan 12 is based on this theme. The plat-form would be modelled in a derelict state, with the former station building converted to some other function. This would probably be an office for a local firm of builders — the conversion to

a private house is unlikely since the railway is still working.

The main point of interest is the use of a sector plate as part of the off-stage trackwork. It not only feeds the two storage roads, but it also replaces the entry points to the run-round loop. This is a very popular arrangement for small compact exhibition layouts with an industrial theme. They are really working dioramas rather than full-blown layouts, but do offer a good deal of scope for the model maker who likes to inject action into his hobby.

This scheme exhibits in a marked form an inconvenience common to most compact branch line designs: like the fisherman's walk, it is a case of two steps and overboard. The train has hardly got going before it has to stop, and while this is acceptable where space is limited, it is always pleasant to see one's trains moving through a stretch of modelled countryside a lit-tle longer than the length of the train.

One approach to the compact ter-minus-fiddle yard branch avoiding this problem was devised by my old friend Maurice Deane. Here the fiddle yard is located immediately behind the sta-tion, hidden from it by a low backscene which can be lifted off when serious operation is taking place. The line goes completely round the layout area and is provided with a short link so that there is a continuous run for testing purposes. His 'Portreath' and 'Culm Valley' branches were the

Plan 12 *Diesel era mineral branch terminus.*
Key:
1 Disused station building; 2 Ground frame; 3 Mineral loading plant; 4 Sector plate.

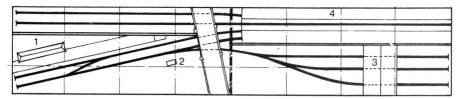

The compact locomotive depot on Alan Wright's 'Cheviotdale' shows how a useful operating facility can be squeezed into a corner that might easily be dismissed as only suitable for scenic development.

inspiration of many modellers, myself included.

Most of Maurice's designs were ultra-compact, but in Plan 13 I have expanded the scheme and added a little more scenic detail to show how this

Plan 13 *Deane pattern branch line layout.*
Key:
1 Station building; 2 Parcels and end loading dock; 3 Cattle loading; 4 Signal cabin; 5 Gasworks; 6 Controls; 7 Goods shed; 8 Coal bins; 9 Offices; 10 Halt; 11 Bridge on lift out section; 12 Loco spur; 13 Kickback siding.

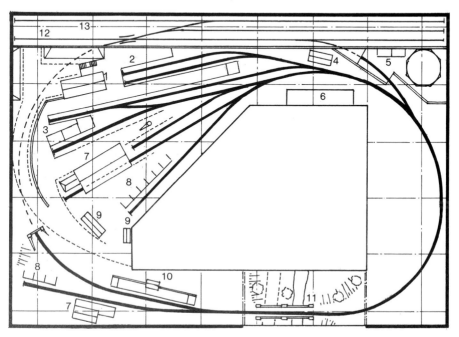

type of layout can be prettied up. The station is very similar in design to Plan 11, with a parcels and end loading dock behind the bay platform. No loco shed is provided. There is a small halt with a siding along the branch, just before it plunges into a tunnel. This is the conventional application, but tunnels are rather rare on branches and so an overbridge could be substituted if so desired. Access to the operating

well is provided by a lift-out section which has a short bridge crossing a valley. Access to the top left corner is a little difficult, so I would be inclined to juggle the tracks and provide an access hatch, covered by a lift-off townscape.

The continuous run is disguised as a spur into the local gasworks. This also allows the gasworks traffic to be more realistic, since the loaded coal

Plan 14 *Cross-country branch junction.*
Key:
1 Station building; 2 Signal cabin; 3 Goods shed; 4 Cattle loading; 5 Ashpit; 6 Coal stage;
7 Water tank; 8 Locomotive shed; 9 Platform shelter; 10 Store shed; 11 Railway cottages.

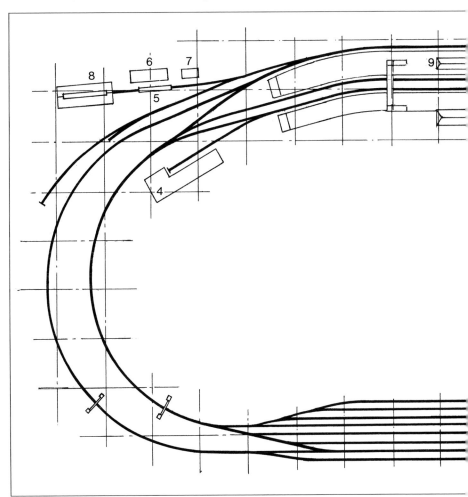

wagons are shunted off-stage and can be replaced by unloaded ones, together with loaded coke wagons to replace the empties that were delivered.

Although the branch line theme was partly promoted as a space-saving exercise, there is no reason why it should not be used where space is no object. Plan 14 occupies, as drawn, a very large area indeed. It is inspired by rather than based on Dulverton on the Devon & Somerset Railway, a Great Western cross-country branch that diverged from the main line at Norton Fitzwarren and terminated at Barnstaple. As it is an imaginative

model, it is pointless to talk of scale, but it is getting within around 80 per cent of the size of this type of station. It can certainly handle the normal length of train found on cross-country branches which is much more to the point.

The basic principle is that the only economical route for the cross-country branch missed the only decent-sized community by several miles. Our ancestors were prone to found settlements in the wrong places. To provide a rail link, a short feeder was laid along the river valley, not altogether convenient but decidedly better than

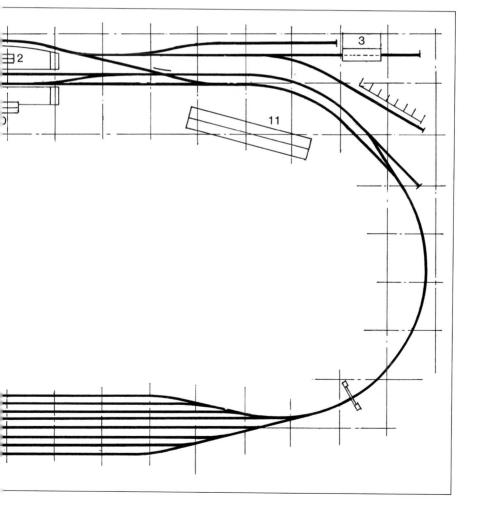

the horse-drawn trap used to get to an inconveniently located station — if indeed you had a trap, for a lot of passengers had to walk the couple of miles to the railway station. They had no option.

The station comprises three loops and two platforms, one of which is a broad island. A small goods yard is provided, which in practice is probably rather more than the station needed, since it is situated in the middle of nowhere. There is a shed for the branch line engine and a siding for the branch set, which is stabled here overnight. There is a central crossover, and a junction feed with single slip to the branch loop which doubles as a goods head-shunt.

Note the row of railway cottages provided for the station staff and the branch engine crew. Whilst by current standards they only offer basic accommodation, they are solidly built and in their time, the late Victorian era, were very desirable properties.

As this is a fairly important station, the buildings are quite extensive. The main station buildings follow the traditional layout, a long building parallel with the platform holding the essential offices, waiting room/ticket office, luggage office, lamp room, porter's room and toilets. At right angles is the integral station house, the residence of the stationmaster, who lived on the job and in practice as well as theory was on 24-hour call-out, though woe betide any minor employee who disturbed him without good cause after working hours.

The hidden loops have eight roads, enough to store sufficient trains to provide a varied service over the line. Ideally, two cross-country trains would meet shortly after the arrival of the shuttle push-pull from the feeder branch. Freight operation could follow two patterns. The pick-up goods along the main branch might only drop any wagons for the nearby town in the yard. These were then picked up by the branch engine and taken down the branch, to be exchanged for others at the terminus. There could also be a through goods train in each direction which conveys wagons along the route without bothering to pick up any local traffic.

An important feature of this type of station is that a very wide selection of locomotive types could be seen on such a route. Single track cross-country routes did occasionally enjoy the luxury of a named train, headed by a powerful express locomotive. If we consider the Somerset & Dorset as falling within this category, then we can justify 'Pacifics' and 2-10-0s.

This scheme has no indication of baseboards or room boundaries because it is essentially a preliminary sketch. It is capable of considerable compression, but equally it is feasible to expand the model by including the branch terminus. There is, as drawn, sufficient room for the branch to climb enough to pass over the main to a station in front of and above the level of the loops.

Another way of exploiting a reasonably large area with the branch line theme is shown in Plan 15. Here the stations are compressed in length, though allowance has been made for four-coach trains. The object has been to fit an OO layout into a standard garage, which can be operated to an intensive timetable by a group of enthusiasts, but which can also be run on a less exacting schedule by the owner and builder.

Plan 15 *Branch line system.*
Key:
1 Station building; 2 Signal cabin; 3 Goods shed; 4 Cattle loading; 5 Coal stage; 6 Ashpit; 7 Water tank; 8 Locomotive shed; 9 Turntable; 10 Controls; 11 Industry; 12 Possible centralized control panel.

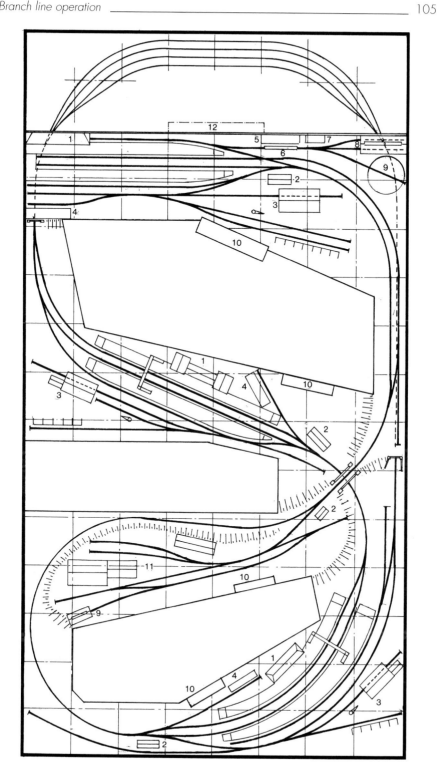

An interesting corner on Alan Wright's 'Cheviotdale'. Storage sidings hold a LNER Sentinel steam railcar, extensively used in the north-east for light local services. The elaborate tunnel mouth is from the Faller kit for the Lorelei tunnels, its monumental architecture quite in keeping with a British scheme. The bolts at the bottom of the photograph secure the lifting flap, used for access into the layout when in its outhouse home.

The main terminus has its run-round loop along the main line. There are three platforms proper, and the shorter bay road is for parcels vans and access to the small loco depot. The yard is adequate for its purpose, containing all the usual facilities.

After the line crosses over the low-level route, we have an extensive rail-linked industry with its own shunting loco. The branch now descends to the junction station where it splits. Taking the major route — the one with two platforms — we pass under the high-level line and enter a major through station with a fairly large goods yard. The line then dives under the terminus to reach a set of storage roads set behind the terminus, from where it runs in tunnel under the high level to reach the junction.

A single operator can deal with the terminus and the through station, controlling the loops in the junction

remotely. The yard at the junction and the industry could not be used. A second operator can take over these stations. Four operators will be able to take over each of the control panels for an intensive session.

It is also possible, at a later stage when an operating group has been established, to install a master control behind the terminus. A strong dais would be needed to give this operator a good view of the entire system. Needless to say, the control circuits would not only need a good deal of planning and take several months to install, but there would also almost inevitably be a long period of debugging needed to get the whole thing working smoothly. This is fine if the owner has a bent for electrification, but it is not a good idea to let an outside expert loose. It is all too likely that just as the rewiring has reached a critical phase, he will change jobs and

Great Central steam railcar arriving at 'Leighton Buzzard' ('Linslade') on Peter Denny's 'Buckingham'.

move away. In one instance, this involved a move to Saudi Arabia — rather far to go for a bit of advice!

CHAPTER 10

The city terminus

There is a natural tendency for enthusiasts to dismiss the city station as being far too big to be suitable for modelling. Of course if you look at the major termini, Euston, Manchester Piccadilly, Glasgow Central and above

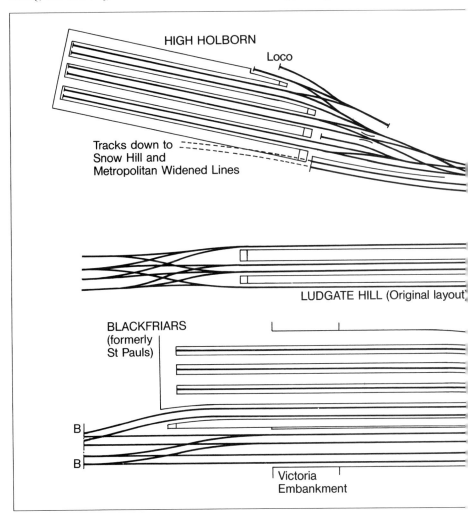

HIGH HOLBORN

Loco

Tracks down to
Snow Hill and
Metropolitan Widened Lines

LUDGATE HILL (Original layout)

BLACKFRIARS
(formerly
St Pauls)

B

B

Victoria
Embankment

all Waterloo, there is reason for this. Yet there are many city stations which are commendably compact and often smaller than their branch line equivalents. Many years ago in the early days of Protofour a part-completed model of Ashburton, built exactly to scale, was shown. It was a very big model indeed and I remarked to the builder that in practically the same space he could have built Charing Cross. 'Oh yes,' he replied. 'Possibly I could, but the operation would have been very limited.'

Nothing could be further from the truth, for as I pointed out in the previous chapter, the smaller branch lines were almost invariably operated by a shuttle train from the junction, and you can't get much more limited than that. A busy city terminus, on the other hand, enjoys a frequent service of both main line and suburban trains, punctuated by parcels, mail and sleeping car trains. Even more to the point, with locomotive-hauled stock, train movements can be extremely complicated, giving one a good reason for owning a large array of different locomotives.

I mentioned Charing Cross as an

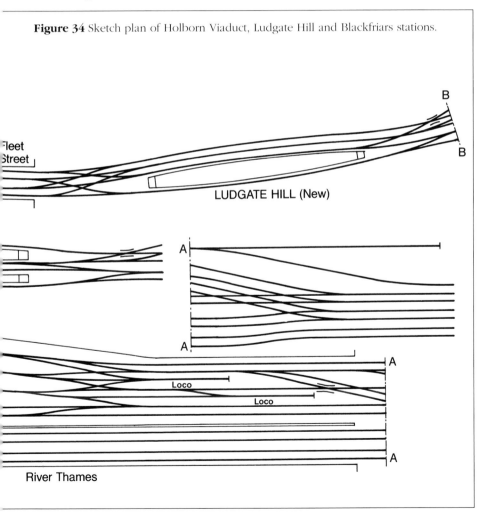

Figure 34 Sketch plan of Holborn Viaduct, Ludgate Hill and Blackfriars stations.

A busy city terminus, modelled by Ron Riddles, long-time Secretary of the Ilford and West Essex MRC.

example of a compact city terminus, though it is by no means the best example of this genre. In London alone there were, in a clockwise direction, Marylebone, Baker Street, Broad Street, Fenchurch Street, Cannon Street, Holborn Viaduct and Blackfriars. Two have departed this world — both Broad Street and Holborn Viaduct have been demolished, but records do exist. Indeed the Blackfriars–Ludgate Hill–Holborn Viaduct complex was a near perfect example of just how close one can squeeze a set of stations, for there was barely a train length between each of them, and the exit pointwork from Ludgate Hill formed the entry throat for Holborn Viaduct. The exact arrangement can be studied in Figure 34. The plans of both Blackfriars and

Holborn Viaduct show the steam age tracks; strictly speaking we should speak of St Paul's rather than Blackfriars, for this was the original name of the station, the only survivor of the trio.

I have not depicted these as a formal track plan since, even in N gauge, the complex would require rather more space than most of us can spare. Any one of the three stations could be used as a basis for a successful model. I would suggest Blackfriars as being the most suitable, if only because the station itself is still there for study. The original station building, a wonderful bit of Victoriana, has been replaced by a bright modern building facing on to the original train shed. The wonderful engraved quoins of the original building are displayed inside, with their evocative list of places you could visit from St Paul's, and even more where it would have been a shade difficult to make a connection. When first I saw them I was tempted to go in and ask the price of a ticket to St Petersburg, echoing unbeknown to me at the time, the comment of Ernest Bevin, one of our greatest Foreign Ministers, who claimed his post-war aim was to be able to go to Victoria and buy a ticket for anywhere he chose.

When I knew the stations all passenger services were in the hands of Southern Railway multiple units, but steam-hauled freight passed over the old spans of Blackfriars Bridge and down the tunnel through Snow Hill and on to the Metropolitan Widened lines, where they could either proceed to Smithfield or go up on to the former LNER at King's Cross or LMS at St Pancras. LMS and LNER locomotives could be seen crossing Blackfriars Bridge as late as the 1950s.

Still in London, I must mention Liverpool Street (Met), the underground station. A recent reconstruction has transformed this busy station. In its heyday it had a terminal road, for many years a turning point of Aylesbury trains hauled by the Metropolitan Railway's named electric locomotives. In its early days, there was a connection to the main Liverpool street, alongside. With pitched overall roof and a bar on the outer rail platform, it had considerable modelling potential,

and was the direct inspiration of my popular 'Minories' scheme for a small city terminus. The original plan was conceived as a terminus for a suburban route, worked entirely by tank locomotives. I had the London, Tilbury and Southend line in mind at the time. Hence no goods facilities were provided. Plan 16 is a variant on the scheme, with a limited goods potential. The passenger section has three platform faces, and a loco spur is arranged so that the loco can run out along the departure track and then back on to whichever train is needed. There is room on the rectangular baseboard shown for extra loco spurs if so desired.

The fourth track is the goods road. From it wagons can be spotted into the covered goods shed, although lack of capacity will ensure that the freight trains will be fairly short. Instead of the conventional release crossover, I have provided a sector plate, a device occasionally employed in this situation. Alternatively a traverser could be used. Two of these were installed in Moor Street, the Great Western suburban terminus in Birmingham, where they remained in use until the end of steam traction on the line.

'Minories' was conceived before diesel traction in Britain had developed beyond the railcar. It was not until long after steam workings had ceased before I realized that it was a perfect station for diesel or electric traction, with both loco-hauled and multiple

Plan 16 *'Minories', a small city terminus.*
Key:
1 Station building (attached to baseboard after erection); 2 Signal cabin; 3 Goods shed; 4 Inspection pit; 5 Sector plate.

unit stock. Indeed, the city terminus is an ideal foundation for such a layout. It can be as simple as 'Minories' or more ambitious, as shown in Plan 17. Here provision is made not only for parcels traffic within the station, but also for modern freight working.

The station has four platforms. A and B are for InterCity trains, with local services concentrated on platform C. Platform D is the parcels road for most of the day, but would take the additional local multiple units during the morning and evening peaks. The station is, of course, a Red Star depot, the offices for which are by the overbridge separating the visual section from the traverser fiddle yard. The signal box is a modern centralized panel governing several miles of track.

Freight is worked in and out of the two roads marked X. After arrival the block trains are backed into the depot through the track marked 4 to a reception yard. In practice, the train simply runs on to the traverser. As no handling facilities are modelled, any type of modern freight traffic can be run.

It would, I think, be a good idea to provide an end loading dock to one of the freight roads. This would allow you to run a car carrier train, and as this involves shunting it is worthwhile. The drill is as follows: initially car transporter wagons are on road X whilst passenger coaches are standing at the end of platform D with the train locomotive attached and another, uncoupled, standing against the buffers. Once the cars have been driven on to the car carriers and the drivers have made their way back to the coaches, these are drawn out of

Plan 17 *Diesel era terminus.*
Key:
1 Station building; 2 Signal cabin; 3 Red Star parcels depot; 4 Track to freight depot; 5 Locomotive standing; 6 Optional section; A-D,X See text.

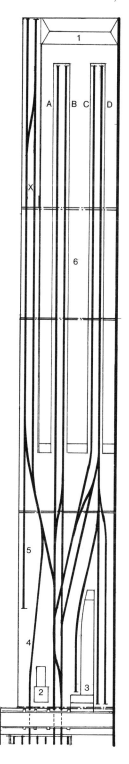

the platform and backed on to the car carriers. Then the train departs. In the fiddle yard it is turned end for end. On its return it goes straight into platform D. A spare locomotive now detaches the car carriers and shunts them into road X in nice time for the drivers to go and remove their vehicles. The spare locomotive now goes back to Platform D and couples on to the coaches. We are now ready to restart the cycle.

As drawn, the station is large enough to take a seven-coach HST set. This will probably make it a shade too large for the layout's site, though easily accommodated in an exhibition hall. The plain section of platforms and tracks marked 6 can be removed to shorten the model without materially affecting its operating pattern.

Our third city terminus, Plan 18, is inspired by the many London termini of the Southern Railway which were on the north bank of the Thames, reached by a long river bridge. The station's main interest lies in the varied platform lengths. There is one long road, a second slightly shorter, then two medium length tracks for local services, and a fifth much shorter road which I envisage as being used primarily for parcels traffic. The shortened platforms provide space for a reasonably sized station building to be provided within the confines of the baseboards. The two loco spurs are put in the only space available; reference back to Blackfriars will show that this is what almost invariably happened.

There are three tracks into the station, one of which leads into the two local platforms and is signalled for

Plan 18 *High-level city terminus.*
Key:
1 Station building; 2 Signal cabin over tracks; 3 Locomotive spurs; 4 Reversible track.

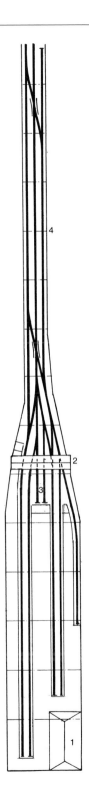

reversible running. In accordance with Southern Region practice, it can be used to stable a spare local train between peak hours. This section can be modelled as a river bridge, preferably with under girders in the style of Cannon Street rather than the high-side girders one sees at Charing Cross. Commercial plastic girders will make short work of this section and reduce the amount of scenic work needed. The over-track signal cabin is introduced for exactly the same reason as the one at Charing Cross — there is nowhere else to put it.

The relative lack of goods facilities at these three stations is deliberate. Furthermore what little there is I intend for van and parcels traffic. This is an aspect of railway operation sadly neglected by modellers until comparatively recently, possibly because of the absence of suitable model vehicles. Happily, there is now a wide selection of suitable models available in 4 mm scale, both ready-to-run and as plastic and etched brass kits. One of the delights of this type of traffic is the sheer variety of types in use, not to mention their longevity. Whereas when a passenger vehicle reaches some 20 years of age, only a complete internal refit makes it acceptable to the customer, parcels and packages are notoriously indifferent to their surroundings, just as long as they keep the rain out.

This type of traffic can be handled at an ordinary platform road in between regular services. Often the platforms needed for commuter trains during the peak hours serve for parcels trains at other times, but on a model it is more fun to provide a separate road for this purpose. Here it is not necessary to ensure that both entry and exit can be carried out without reversal, so there is a chance to include a deliberate snarl.

Although I have spoken of parcels traffic as forming separate trains, parcels vehicles can be attached to passenger trains. Other additions were the passenger-rated freight stock, which have to be removed from the core rake of coaches, unlike pure parcels vehicles which frequently formed part of the main train formation and remained attached for the return working. These were often described as guards vans, but not all parcels vans contain accommodation for the train staff, a point that should be carefully watched by the discerning modeller, since to send out a passenger train without a guard's compartment prior to the 1980s is one of the most heinous operating errors one can commit.

There is a general belief that the guard travels in the last vehicle. This was the case in the days before continuous brakes, when a train might carry several men rated as guards, with the senior guard riding in the last coach or van. In practice he was the guard, he was responsible for the proper working of the train, and the rest were brakesmen who screwed down the brakes on their coach when the driver whistled. Many railways fitted two whistles, one for normal use, the other a signal to apply brakes immediately. The Great Western Railway and Western Region continued this practice to the end of steam for reasons best known to the railways' officers. The advent of the continuous brake, which could be applied by driver or guard and, in a partial form, by any passenger who had reason to pull what was still termed the communication cord, allowed one man to serve the train and freed him from his post at the rear. However, the vans were generally kept at one end of the train as relatively few gangwayed vans were provided with cages to separate passengers from parcels traffic. BR standard brake seconds were so provided, but it was only quite late in the story that they were put in the middle of long-distance stopping trains, where they were best positioned for traffic purposes.

Having gone into the peripheral traffic, it is high time we considered the main purpose of the city station, passenger trains. These came in every conceivable variety, and are obviously the real reason why such a station should be the first choice of the operator. The core traffic fell into two main groups. First and foremost is the local service, usually formed from non-corridor compartment stock with slam doors hauled by tank locomotives. These trains ran throughout the day often on a regular interval basis with up to four trains an hour plus extras at peak periods. Long-distance trains left at irregular times for various destinations, the great majority making stops at intermediate points along the route. In addition there were the principal expresses. These were normally named and had restaurant cars included in the formation, but it was not until comparatively late that some form of refreshment service was available on every train but the refreshment rooms could supply packed meals. These began as elaborately presented affairs in wicker baskets, often including a bottle of wine, and ended as packs of sandwiches and fruit in cardboard cartons.

There was one vital difference between the local and long-distance service in the steam age. The former were turned round in the terminal roads and were lucky if they saw a carriage cleaner other than at night. The coaches that formed principal expresses were normally worked out of the station by a shunting locomotive and taken to the carriage sidings where they would be cleaned throughout with varying degrees of attention to detail, the header tanks for the lavatories refilled and the destination boards changed. The train formation might be altered. The GWR was particularly prone to do this, but all companies added or removed coaches, the ideal being a standard formation which could be strengthened by the addition of extra coaches. These were usually older stock kept to hand for this purpose. Only the prestige express trains, frequently made up of specially designed coaches for that service, remained as standard sets.

From the turn of the century onward, many prestige expresses ran a considerable distance non-stop. To provide for those who did not want to go all the way, these were often followed closely by a secondary express which made several stops and, on longer journeys, took anything up to an hour longer to make the trip. The service was also useful when the named train was filled to capacity, when late-comers without seat reservations were directed to the relief train. Indeed, in the steam age relief trains were very common on summer Saturdays, while some trains were run in two or three portions. Another feature of larger steam age termini was the separation of the platform roads into arrival and departure. This can be well worth reproducing in model form, because it not merely provides an extra shunt movement, but can simplify the entry pointwork considerably.

In the early days, the large glazed train sheds at termini served two purposes, to keep rain off passengers and to provide covered overnight storage for coaches. Many began with just two platforms, the intervening space being occupied by sidings which as traffic grew were removed in favour of more platforms. Some platform roads were provided with release crossovers, as on branches, but generally these were fed on to central roads so that it was not necessary to clear one platform before releasing the locomotive. In practice, these roads were found more useful for holding spare coaches and vans, it being more convenient to put another locomotive on to the rear of the train. On a model railway, it is, I think, best to omit release crossovers at large termini, not only to save on points, but also to increase the effective capacity of the station and make each platform road a useful storage siding. Furthermore, if an overall roof is fitted it is more convenient to arrange for automatic uncoupling of the original train locomotive than to try to juggle with it under the glazing. Where three-link couplings are preferred, the simple knock-off trip on the locomotive, described in Chapter 3, coupled with a fixed spring decoupler in the platform road, detaches the locomotive in a positive manner. Tension lock couplings are best dealt with by a very long sprung ramp. I would suggest that Perspex is best for the ramp, since it will be virtually invisible under the roof.

An important feature of major city stations was — and is — that the main area is devoted to passengers, parcels and mail traffic and that few, if any, servicing facilities are provided, these being located some distance along the line. This separation of facilities is rarely modelled, yet it has many distinct advantages. There is of course the fact that if the model is constructed on sectional baseboards, one may begin with the passenger terminus, which feeds almost directly into the fiddle yard, and then add the locomotive servicing facilities, the goods yard and the carriage sidings stage by stage. While it will be possible for one operator to make use of these, clearly the model will now call for several operators, and although remaining just one station complex, will be a fully fledged operating system. Furthermore, the operating pattern at each section will be completely different, not only giving the regular gang a chance to rotate

This diesel era terminus in 7 mm scale shows the potential of the city terminus in a relatively small space. A two-car DMU stands in the bay road whilst a three-coach loco-hauled train has just arrived at the main platform. Car carrier traffic was catered for at the end loading dock on the right.

Pioneer LMS main line diesel No 10000 at the head of a parcels train at 'Tamerig Central'. One of two locomotives built at the very end of the grouped era, the prototype has attracted little attention from modellers.

duties, but also providing at least one fairly stress-free area for the newcomer.

Modern British operation follows a different pattern. For a start, all local services which have not been axed are worked by multiple unit stock, diesel or electric. Passenger services are increasingly following the same path, first with the HST, later with the electric push-pull trains on the East and West Coast services. It might seem that operation would be very dull indeed.

In practice this need not be the case, providing you do not move fully into the post-1990 era. On the local side, using diesel railcar sets, there is the possibility of splitting a set. A very interesting move is where two units arrive coupled together and are then split to two sections to work to different destinations. With loco-hauled stock there is the question of both air-conditioned stock and air brakes, requiring the use of the appropriate diesel on the train, a subtle but interesting feature of train working from the mid-1970s to the late 1980s. The

ready availability of British Rail coaches in varying marks and different patterns makes it much easier to assemble prototypical trains without having to resort to extensive kit construction or else put up with a brake second — first/second formation.

Whatever the merits of sectorization may be on the prototype, in model form one cannot praise it too highly, for not only does it add a very welcome splash of colour to the scene, it also gives a good reason for owning far more locomotives than you strictly need, which is definitely a good thing. It also provides a perfect way of dividing the serious operator, who will get the right loco on the right train — except in emergencies — from the man with a toy train mentality who either doesn't care, or more likely, just doesn't know why the locos are in different colours — even though the makers' catalogues tell you.

The switch from all-purpose to block trains on the freight side simplifies operation. The block freight train first saw extensive use on operating layouts, where a fixed formation not merely eliminated shunting, but also reduced the size of the goods yard dramatically since a single siding sufficed. Modern operating practice has just caught up with this.

When, in the late '50s, diesels were taking over from steam and lines were closing in a wholesale fashion, many people began to talk gloomily of the demise of the hobby through lack of prototype inspiration. I never subscribed to this view, nor did Sydney Pritchard, which is why we coined the term *modern image* to promote the theme. Personally, I always thought that the double bogie diesel or electric loco, which doesn't need turning and is much happier on sharp curves than any steam locomotive, has a lot going for it. As the drive for efficiency gained momentum (in practice, making railwaymen redundant and cutting out frills), it became increasingly obvious that the prototype was adopting, usually in a more sophisticated form, operating practices we had long used to allow one man to carry out the work of an entire station staff. Modern railways are tremendous fun to work in model form. It is a pity that this book is being written before the Channel Tunnel is open and before there is any extensive involvement of private operators on British Rail. Whatever one's opinion of this last move might be, there is little doubt in my mind that it will provide model operators with a fresh opportunity to introduce variety into their operating pattern. One thing is absolutely certain: our railways have never been more colourful.

Before we leave the subject, I offer another popular layout design, the central terminus with a triangular junction to a multi-track main line. Plan 19 will fit into a garage in 4 mm scale and as well as a large terminus with a good range of facilities provides a long, rel-

atively uncluttered stretch of main line on which trains can be seen running in their natural habitat. However, before I deal with this part of the layout, we can look at the station itself.

On the passenger side there are no less than six platform faces of differing lengths. At least one of the outside faces would be mainly used for parcels traffic. With every platform of a slightly different length, matching the right train to the right road will call for a good deal of care during operation. At the same time there is a differentiation between the express and semi-fast trains, with between five- and seven-coach formations, and the local three- and four-coach sets. The platform roads will also serve as off-peak carriage sidings, a common practice on the prototype.

Goods traffic is well catered for. There are two tracks for coal traffic on one side and three for general merchandise on the other, while the bay platform can probably be used to hold spare vehicles during shunting sessions.

A small motive power depot is included, with the three functions separated. Coaling and valeting is carried out on the turntable roads, the shed is used solely for storage, and there are two cripple roads, one equipped with a set of sheer legs to allow locomotives to be lifted clear of a pair of wheels for attention to the main bearings.

Outside the station, the line diverges and links to form a triangular junction.

Plan 19 *Terminus with triangular junction to four-track main line.*
Key:
1 Station building; 2 Signal cabin; 3 Goods shed; 4 Ashpit; 5 High-level coal stage with water tank over; 6 Turntable; 7 Locomotive shed; 8 Sheer legs; 9 Main controls; 10 Passenger sub-controls; 11 Locomotive shed sub-controls; 12 Main line controls.

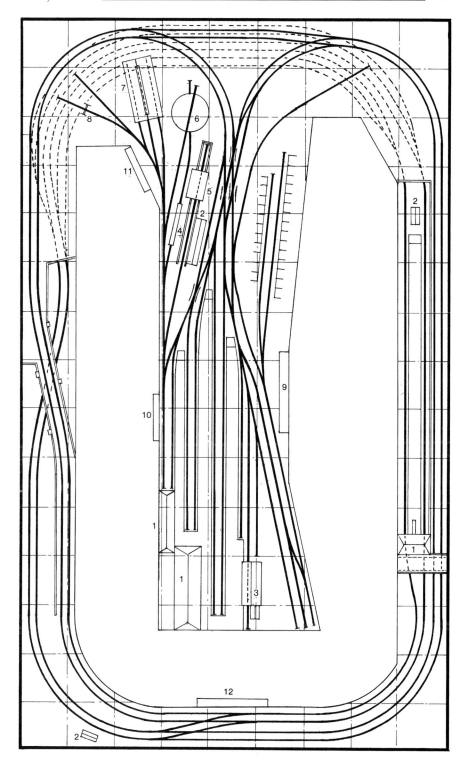

'West Road' station is a good example of a well-equipped city terminus based on BR (Eastern) practice, with three platforms and reasonable goods facilities.

The further road is solely to allow continuous running and could well be omitted as a pair of crossovers at the far end allow limited continuous running if desired. The main tracks are laid out as a complete spiral so that a train will make two complete circuits of the system before returning to base. As it passes through the hidden loops under the upper junction, with three loops on both clockwise and anti-clockwise circuits, the sequence of trains can be adjusted to provide a varied operating schedule.

The simple through station might appear to have no operating significance. Nothing could be further from the truth, for it allows you to differentiate between local and express passenger services during operation. Only the former will stop, the latter will run clear through. This is surprisingly satisfying and adds immeasurably to the illusion we are striving to achieve, that we are running real trains on a real railway.

This layout is not too onerous for a lone enthusiast to build and maintain. It is not a particularly difficult layout to construct, and is well within the reach of a determined newcomer. It would cost about as much as a fortnight's holiday for two in an exotic location. In addition to the extensive array of track and the numerous turnouts, including a battery of slip points, it requires a considerable amount of rolling stock and a generous locomotive stud. It would probably be best to consider this type of model when the collection has reached the point where it demands a layout of this nature to show it to advantage.

The layout can be controlled by one man. I suggest the ideal spot is alongside the goods yard, since movement of locomotives in and out of the MPD is easier to carry out at a distance. As the operating well is one continuous passageway, the operator can walk round the central island to get at the other side. I have indicated where sub-panels might be located to control the passenger section, the MPD and the main line when friends are around to help run the model. It is possible to combine station working, watching the trains go by and timetable operation in any preferred proportion on this one comparatively straightforward layout. There is not a lot of scope for scenic development, though in many modellers' opinion multiple tracks on a relatively narrow baseboard need little embellishment. Of course, with a railway room some 10 to 15 per cent larger, the same plan could be opened up to advantage. Larger radii for the curves, an extension of platform length to take longer trains and more space to site the main line tracks in open countryside would improve the model enormously without materially adding to the workload.

CHAPTER 11
System operation

Single-handed operation of a model railway is something of a contradiction in terms, for the essence of full-size railway working is the team-work of a number of individuals. The lone wolf can operate a single station satisfactorily, he can watch trains travel majestically through model scenery, he can even exercise control over several satellite stations from a centralized panel. These are excellent goals, they provide satisfaction and enjoyment in no small measure but there is no gainsaying the fact that the ultimate enjoyment of the hobby is only achieved when two or more enthusiasts get together for a running session.

I have shown that it is possible, indeed desirable, to design a large system so that it can be operated by one man. I have also shown how on all but the most elementary of layouts it is equally possible to make provision for a second operator. If anything this needs more stress than the fairly obvious point that it's a good idea to be able to get at least a limited service running at any given moment. Just as in full size the object is to run trains from point to point, on a model layout trains are exchanged between operators according to a set of mutually agreed rules.

While an operating group is useful on a small layout, particularly if it is intended for exhibition display, on a large layout it is essential if the full potential of the layout is to be enjoyed.

It is not merely that several operators are wanted to man the various control panels; there are other features where numbers count. Although certain core tasks have to be carried out in the railway room, a lot of work on a model railway is more conveniently performed elsewhere. Locomotives, rolling stock and buildings are traditionally assembled and maintained in a separate workshop. With a group these jobs are frequently spread around. These points are not difficult to grasp, but to the uninitiated there appears to be an insuperable difficulty. Desirable as a group of fellow workers might be, one can hardly walk into a model shop and order an operating group. Or can you?

If we look at successful system layouts, the operating team has frequently coalesced without advertising or conscious recruiting. A large, interesting layout is a proven attraction and keen operators who are prepared to travel considerable distances to enjoy a well-organized running session soon discover its existence. Of course, the builder needs to let it be known that such a layout is under construction. One place to do this is the specialist model shop, the place where kindred spirits foregather to chat as well as buy models and equipment. The local model railway club is another fruitful recruiting ground. Less obvious but, in my experience, equally effective meeting places are pubs and church groups, or indeed any social organization that has a broad intake is a likely place to meet others who share your interests. For every individual with the resources and drive needed to create an interesting model railway, there are at least half a dozen others who would like to do the same, but who for one reason or another cannot get started. They are only too happy to share the work. They only need pointing in the right direction.

There is also the possibility of forming a club to build a large joint layout, a system that appears to work well everywhere but in Britain. This is probably because the existing club structure in Britain is built around an annual exhibition rather than a common layout, and aims at a fairly large membership with relatively low dues. Club layouts are designed to be easily trans-

ported to an exhibition and operated by a very small team. Clubrooms are usually rented on short leases and the probability of having to move at short notice is accepted as an inevitable hazard. Above all, such clubs not only run regular recruiting campaigns, but will accept anyone who pays his or her subscription. Furthermore, it is taken for granted that not only will over half the membership make no contribution to the club other than their annual subscription, but a sizeable proportion will never attend more than one meeting a year, if that.

A group formed to build a layout needs to be small, with every member an active contributor to the construction and maintenance of the layout. Membership is a privilege, not a right, and numbers are normally limited to 10 or less, compared with the 20-plus

Norman Eagles operating Oxton *on his 'Sherwood' section, seen here in its penultimate form in a loft in Pinner. The line was run with clockwork locomotives and hands-on operation meant just that.*

of the general purpose club. Subscriptions are high, for in addition to the rental of a suitable site, with a long, renewable lease which has been carefully checked for nasty break clauses, there is the cost of the layout's substructure, track and scenery. It is normally the case that members provide the bulk of the locomotives and rolling stock, but in several well-known cases even these are owned by the group. Ideally, the written constitution should be drafted by a lawyer, since the ownership of a valuable joint asset must be clearly defined. Above all, the important layout parameters, scale, gauge, overall design and prototype followed must be agreed at the outset and written into the constitution in such a manner that it is obvious that they cannot be changed on a whim.

Whereas the normal British club is extremely democratic and informal, a layout-oriented club must be an autocracy. The autocrat is not one strong-willed individual, but the layout itself. This is why its parameters need to be defined in a formal document, copies of which are in the possession of every member and available for inspection by any interested individual or prospective new member.

Where the layout is begun by someone who happens to have space for a decent-size layout, many problems disappear. For a start, there is greater security of tenure, there is also no question of disagreement over scale, gauge, track standards, overall level of detail and scale accuracy and, above all, of period and prototype. These are determined by the ground landlord who is automatically the final court of appeal.

Perhaps the most successful of such groups was the Sherwood Gang, the operating group who ran Norman Eagles' O gauge 'Sherwood', an extensive system that represented an imaginary section of the old LMS in 1938.

The layout was steadily developed for over 60 years and although it was finally dismantled after the death of Norman Eagles, the group retains its identity and will exist until the last member passes away.

Much of the success of the 'Sherwood' system was due to the underlying organization. Every facet of the layout was under the personal direction of a gaffer, a member who happened to have the necessary expertise and interest in the specific subject to undertake responsibility for that part of the layout. As the layout developed, this system underwent changes, the most significant of which occurred when 'Sherwood' moved from Pinner to Saunderton, and the layout, which had been located in the loft, was re-erected in a large industrial pattern timber building at the end of the garden. Reconstruction took a couple of years, during which time members were busily engaged first in preparing the site, then erecting the building, installing lighting and heating before work could begin on re-erecting the layout.

Several temporary gaffers were appointed, the most important of whom was the track planning gaffer, who had to produce a scheme that retained the original concept and as much as possible of the original layout while exploiting the greater space now available for the model. This was a great success. In its final form 'Sherwood' provided amusement and entertainment not only for the Gang, now spread over most of the Home Counties, but also for many friends who were entertained at the monthly running sessions throughout the spring, summer and autumn months.

I have deliberately not given details of the 'Sherwood' organization since its form was not only set by the layout itself, but also by the membership of the Gang. A different line with different

Nottingham Castle, the principal terminus of 'Sherwood'. This photograph was taken in the line's Jubilee year when the railway was housed in a large industrial pattern timber building at the end of the garden in Saunderton.

people would want to set up a system based on its own needs and abilities. The important point is that every member of the group should have an understood role in the organization. Whether this is part of a relatively rigid hierarchal system or a looser association is entirely up to the group. The important point is to remember that operating a model railway is a team game.

It is not at all fanciful to draw comparison with sport. If you want to play football, you have first to decide which code you are going to follow. There are plenty to choose from, each with differing rules and methods of play. Whilst adherents of any particular code will assure you of its superiority and be surprised if you beg to differ, there isn't a lot to choose between any of them when one considers the important matter, sheer enjoyment.

Having agreed on the code, you then need to choose a team and decide the position of the players. Team members do not necessarily have to play in the same position each game, nor does the team always have

to consist of the same 11 players. At this point the analogy breaks down. You don't need a referee, because operating a layout is not competitive; nor is it necessary to have training sessions away from the layout. However, the fundamental principle remains true. If half are playing to one code and half to another, if anyone feels free to change the rules part way through the game, if someone decides to walk out at a crucial moment, you get a chaotic situation whether you are playing football or trains.

It is necessary for newcomers to learn the ropes, particularly if they have no experience of being part of a multi-operator organization. Even those with extensive experience in this field need at the very least a brief acclimatization lecture and a chance to familiarize themselves with the track layout and controls of the section they are expected to operate. The closer the layout conforms to prototype operating practice, the more important it becomes for operators to know and understand the agreed procedures. It might seem that anyone familiar with

Gretley Colliery was the major source of coal on 'Sherwood'. Even in the greater space of the Saunderton building, it still had a very cramped site, with only one shaft and winding gear and a single two-track loading shed.

full-size practice ought to be able to take over on such layouts at a moment's notice. Unfortunately, it is rarely possible to simulate every facet of prototype operation, and the omissions, simplifications and compromises adopted on any practical working model railway make it necessary for a stranger to go warily on his or her initial stint at the controls.

In an ideal world a training programme for newcomers would involve a preliminary study of the group's operating rules, but in our less than perfect society such rules are all too often unwritten. I am not going to suggest that a written code is essential. Indeed, it calls for a member with the skill to write a clear, unambiguous document and another with the tact to get everyone to agree. The usual procedure is to put the novice to work on the least demanding panel on the layout and see how he gets on with it. This seems to work well enough, since the newcomer absorbs the ethos of the group whilst enjoying himself as an operator.

In many USA clubs, operators wear engineer's caps. To outsiders this appears at best an amiable eccentricity. It isn't, because in the well-organized groups you don't get to wear the cap until you've passed out as a competent operator. There is good reason in any group where high standards are set for making some sort of presentation to new members who achieve this level. We all appreciate acknowledgment of our expertise and cherish hard-won diplomas.

Which brings me to a very important point. Several well-known layout operating groups are regularly criticized for their apparent exclusive nature. I've known many of them very well, and into the bargain known some of the more vociferous critics. I've tried on many occasions to explain why this is so and, indeed, must be so.

For a start, a layout group needs to limit its membership to the number experience shows is sufficient to operate and maintain the model. It is not merely that there is no room for passengers: there is no place for supernumeraries who must inevitably feel

Bob Ledger's large 7 mm scale operating layout is set on the Midland Railway in Lancashire running to the Manchester Central terminus. For exhibition work it is worked in real time to an hourly timetable in strict accordance with prototype practice. Here we can see the outer end of the line beyond Chinley station. On the left is Rowsley Sidings, the exhibition yard which replaces a reverse loop. On the right a large engine shed has been added for the exhibition. The time is right on the hour; the service will soon restart with the departure of the goods from the nearest line. This will be followed by the parcels train and the DMU in the background on a Sheffield–New Mills short working. The fourth train is an ICI limestone train from Tunstead Quarry. Photo: Nick Freezer

left out of the fun. In addition, every member needs to be able to contribute positively to the group in one way or another. Even more important, the group must be compatible. There is no room for the outsider who thinks he knows how the group should be run. He may be right, that it would be possible to do things differently and perhaps improve on certain facets of the layout. However, the existing group are satisfied with things as they are, and it's their layout.

In my experience even the most exclusive organizations are happy to admit people they like as associates, and to offer them the chance to become full members in due course. That this involves, at the outset, tackling the less pleasant tasks, like sweeping up, putting things away in their proper places, making tea or coffee and the like is only following a long-standing principle in society. You have to earn your place in any worthwhile organisation. Groucho Marx summed it up very neatly when he told an organization that was trawling for members (and charging them heavily for the privilege), 'I wouldn't join a club that would have me for a member.'

CHAPTER 12
Exhibition working

Although in theory any layout that is reasonably easy to dismantle, transport some distance and re-erect in a couple of hours is a potential exhibition layout, rather more is required of it if it is to entertain and enthuse the visitor. Obviously, it needs to have a modicum of scenic treatment and so present a pleasing picture to the viewer. It should work reliably, that is understood. Most important of all, it should be operated according to a pre-determined plan so that the interested viewer can see that the workings of a railway have also been modelled.

There are those who say loudly and often that the public only come to see trains running and therefore the out-and-out tail chaser, where trains dash past every 10 seconds or so, is the

The Gauge 1 Model Railway Association have a large joint layout which is now a popular fixture at IMREX every Easter. The layout is assembled from units on site every year and differs slightly on each occasion. With plenty of live steam locomotives, as well as electrically powered models, it is normally surrounded three deep by visitors avidly watching the trains go by. This photograph shows it in the 1950s in the basement at the Central Hall.

The Model Railway Club's 4 mm scale 'New Annington' is a popular feature of IMREX. We see it here in its early days, before the overhead wires went up on the main line. Ian Wood is at the old master panel (now moved into the centre of the layout), whilst Nick Freezer is controlling the trains on the far right.

only appropriate type of layout for an exhibition. This is dangerous nonsense, for it ignores the fact that straw polls have shown repeatedly that when asked how they discovered the show was on, over half the visitors mention a model railway magazine. Furthermore, whatever interests the enthusiast will also entertain the typical visitor. More to the point, by showing the uninitiated that a model railway can be run just like the real thing, there is a far better chance of converting their casual interest into something more concrete.

It is understood that everything should have been tested beforehand; the layout itself should be in good order and there should be enough spare locomotives, coaches and wagons to hand over and above those needed to run the model, so that a suspect runner can be replaced instantly. This, however, is only the start. Although the layout can be easily run single-handed at home, a minimum of two operators is needed at a one-day show. It is not merely that

you need a break for meals and refreshment. You will want to look at the other layouts and visit the trade stands while you're there.

One solution is to have a small support group. This is the case with club layouts and with some privately owned layouts. The group, who may well have helped build the layout and may also be providing some of the stock, will be familiar with the controls and will also know how the timetable works. Ideally, they will have rehearsed the operating schedule many times before.

Unfortunately, this is not an ideal world, and come to that it is not always convenient to have a support group for a small private layout. Fortunately, within the hobby there are plenty of experienced operators who are prepared to lend a hand, some of whom are capable of coming to a strange layout and taking over the control at a moment's notice and putting on a polished performance. However, one should never leave things to chance. There is a simple method of providing any intelligent person with the information needed to run a layout in accordance with a timetable, although he or she knows absolutely nothing about railways, model or full size: the flip card which was described in Chapter 6. It is possible to operate a timetable at an exhibition without flip cards; it is also possible to push a pea up Mount Snowdon with your nose. I'd not recommend either course.

Most railway modellers are familiar with Murphy's Law, which in its general case states *if something can go wrong, it will.* There is a sub-clause which adds that *during demonstrations, everything will fail.* Therefore, there are two essential adjuncts to an exhibition layout, a well-equipped toolbox and some spare stock, which must include at least two spare locos for every day the show is open. It cannot be over-emphasized that it is next-door to impossible to carry out repair and maintenance while operating a working layout. Many large club lay-

outs allocate one individual as maintenance staff and provide a small portable workbench, while others run demonstration stands where operators can take defective locomotives for proper overhaul.

Murphy also points out that power sockets are never located in a convenient place. A lengthy extension lead is a useful addition to the exhibition kit, as is a four-way adaptor. Thankfully one is unlikely to encounter a non-standard socket in a public hall, and so the universal flat pin plug will serve. A reel of self-adhesive parcel tape, a reel of Sellotape, preferably on a dispenser, and a ball of string will get you out of many a hole, while a staple gun is so useful you must have your name on yours, as everyone else will want to borrow it. Blu-tack and drawing pins also come in handy, and finally it does help to have a supply of stiff card and felt tip pens, plus a set of stencils so that you can put up a notice on demand.

This brings us to the question of presentation. For a start, lighting in

Chinley station on Bob Ledger's 7 mm scale layout in 1979. It is eight minutes past the hour and as the local from Manchester Central to Derby is signalled away on the up slow line, on the left an LMS Compound has come off shed and is waiting for the signal to run to Rowsley Sidings. Photo: Nick Freezer

public halls is rarely good. All too frequently it verges on the Stygian, and layout lighting is essential. It is not merely that visitors want to see the models; the operators need to be able to do so. A couple of adjustable domestic spotlights on vertical poles will suffice, but if the layout is to go on to the exhibition circuit in a serious way, a fascia which not only supports the lighting, but also displays the name of the layout is a better solution.

The fascia can also carry the logos of any group or society to which the layout owner belongs, and it is not, I think, at all pretentious to add one's name, albeit in smaller lettering. Obviously the lettering needs to be of a professional standard, but there is no need to employ a sign-writer since most good office or artist's suppliers can provide large self adhesive letters, if not from stock then certainly to order. A little professional polish adds to the prestige of the layout and confers distinction to the exhibition.

By the same token, it is helpful to provide viewers with as much information about the working as possible. This not only informs the knowledgeable viewer, but it also shows the casual visitor that the layout is working to a timetable or some sort of sequence. There are two fairly simple arrangements possible, each involving a large display board above the layout. Figure 35 shows how this can be done with the timetable fully set out and a clock placed alongside giving layout time.

Alternatively, there is the train describer. This has a series of lights placed alongside the descriptions of the trains that are running on the lines of Figure 36. The best arrangement is to provide slotted holders for thin card notices rather than painted descriptions on a plain board. Not only are these easier to change but it is also relatively simple to make a good job of the display using a set of stencils.

Another possibility is to run the service in step with a tape commentary. This is not as difficult as it sounds, for the tape is not prepared until the schedule has been thoroughly rehearsed and the commentary is deliberately stretched to give a little extra time over and above that actually needed, which makes the actual operating a little less fraught. There are audible prompts, and the pace is more leisurely as the commentary covers the pauses to keep to time. There are two very real difficulties, the first of which being the need to make a polished tape recording, for much of the effect is lost if the commentary is obviously the work of an amateur. The second and even more serious objection is that while commentaries are popular with visitors they are less than popular with other exhibitors. Should there be two

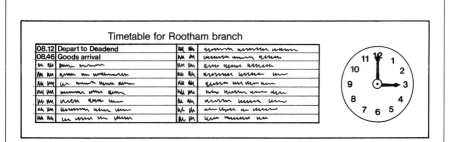

Figure 35 *Timetable display and layout clock.*

UP EXPRESS TO LONDON

DOWN EXPRESS FROM LONDON

UP LOCAL PASSENGER

DOWN LOCAL PASSENGER

UP PICK-UP GOODS

DOWN PICK-UP GOODS

SPECIAL TRAIN

Isometric sketch
showing removeable
train boards

Figure 36 *Train describer.*

A busy scene around the Fleischmann layout at EUFMO, 1981. The Fleischmann layouts are automatic in operation and frequently incorporate elaborate train movements. At this time these were controlled entirely by banks of bi-stable relays actuated by track contacts. Whilst technically interesting, the object was to eliminate operator control, rather than provide operational interest. This is the ultimate in watching the trains go by, and ideally suited for exhibition.

such layouts in one hall, the resulting cacophony is all but unbearable.

Communication with the visitor, while desirable, is not essential. Communication between operators is most definitely essential, and block bells (which are covered in Chapter 13) should be mandatory under exhibition conditions. They have the great advantage of being quite distinctive and can be readily heard against the general hubbub of a busy show. Headsets and microphones are very useful. What should be ruled out is a direct shout, which is not only unprofessional, it also often leads to misunderstanding.

Some exhibition organizers try to stop eating and drinking behind layouts, though how such a ban can be enforced is a mystery, since there are few sanctions one can apply to volunteers whose active co-operation is needed for the smooth functioning of the show. On the other hand, many shows now make a point of bringing regular supplies of tea and coffee to all stands, recognizing that operating is thirsty work. I do, however, feel that eating is best done away from the layout, but this is mainly because I feel that operators need a break.

There are a few things well worth including in the exhibition pack: a tray for collecting drinks, a clean towel and a small bar of soap in a container. Yes, public halls do have lavatories, but very few have either soap or clean towels left halfway through the afternoon. Indigestion and headache tablets and a pack of plasters are also worth including. Hopefully you won't need them, but if you do you will want them immediately. You may well ask what has this to do with operation? Everything, for if the operator is below par, running will suffer out of all proportion.

CHAPTER 13
Block bells and communication

Anyone who has attended several model railway exhibitions and spent any appreciable time watching the working layouts in operation will have seen plenty of cases where either a train comes to an abrupt stop in the middle of its journey or has taken the wrong road at a facing turnout and has had to be backed ignominiously out of a siding. With any luck he will have witnessed at least one case where a train is sent into an occupied section with hilarious results — at least as far as the viewer is concerned. While such incidents are quite common on unorganized layouts, they do sometimes happen on layouts where there is a

The main line junction serving a feeder branch provides a wealth of action, since a varied pattern of main line services are supplemented by the connecting branch trains. At 'Combe Mellin' this is emphasized by the nameboards, which instruct passengers to change for the branch and main line respectively. These are delightfully vague, for whilst conforming to GWR practice in layout, they do not follow the actual pattern of wording, which was always specific, naming not only the branch terminus, but also the principal main line destinations. London was almost invariably mentioned. It is worth adding that on occasions the towns mentioned were only served by bus. This happened when the service had originally been provided by the railway company.

proper timetable controlled by flip cards.

While the direct cause can be any one of a dozen things, the underlying reason is the fact that, on a model railway, decisions need to be made in a flash. Even on a large layout, a train will take less than 30 seconds to run from one station to another. In most instances, an entire train movement is completed within 10 seconds. There is no time to abort an incorrect move before it is obvious to the most casual observer that someone has made a mistake. Under these conditions it is essential to know that everything is in order *before* the train is set into motion.

On the face of it, it is not difficult. A clear road is set up, the necessary section switches are thrown and the operator then drives the train to its destination. Since one individual is responsible for everything, setting the road, energizing the sections and driving the train, it is reasonably straightforward. While this might seem restricted to relatively simple layouts with just one operator, it also applies where walk-around control is used. Of course, with this system there is the ever-present possibility that two operators may want to occupy the same section.

This is where a properly compiled timetable comes to the rescue, since one of the most important objects of timetable compilation is to ensure that you do not get two trains trying to occupy the same space at the same time. Of course in a less than perfect world things can go wrong, and so the operating rules should lay down in advance who has priority. The American system works as well on the model as it does in full size. Trains are categorized, passenger takes precedence over freight, expresses take priority over locals. Should two trains of equal status meet then the direction of travel is taken into account. This is a simplification of a fairly complex concept, but the essence is that priorities and protocols are written down beforehand.

This principle is equally important when the layout is controlled from several fixed positions. Most problems arise when two or more people who are working together omit to decide in advance who does what. This applies whether the operators have equal status or there is an hierarchal system in force where one individual is the chief controller.

This last arrangement is needed when the section switches are concentrated in a single main panel, corresponding to a centralized control box on the prototype. Here the drivers should obey the working signals, and providing the controller knows what he is about, everything should proceed in an orderly fashion. This arrangement requires working signals, clearly visible to the operator. As this is rarely possible, repeaters should be provided so that the operators are able to see that the road is clear.

The central controller needs to be able to see most of what is going on. Normally this is done by placing the controls on a raised dais so that he can get a bird's eye view of the proceedings. It is usually necessary to provide a few strategically located mirrors to enable him to look round corners. With the advent of relatively inexpensive closed circuit TV monitors, this hi-tec option is growing in favour. Although the definition is usually indifferent, it is possible to see the position of trains on the hidden parts of the layout with sufficient clarity.

The individual operators are in the position of drivers and, since they do not have to operate points or signals, are happier with a hand-held controller on a long lead. Anyone with a basic knowledge of railway working can take over control of a train with no

Even where the main operating interest lies in the station, it is helpful to have a short stretch of unencumbered main line where one can simply watch the trains go by. This section is clearly ripe for scenic development. In order to preserve maximum visibility, a cutting, viaduct or, as in this example, a river bridge is to be preferred. This intriguing model uses two girder bridge and one turntable kit, together with some scratch-built piers to create a distinctive feature. Pity about the canal narrow boat; it doesn't quite fit into an otherwise nicely observed slice of imaginative modelling.

more than five minutes' instruction and a short period, say a quarter of an hour, spent watching the layout, learning the road. When signal repeaters or a full illuminated panel for the operators are provided, driving trains is unalloyed delight. It is a very good simulation of full-size railway working, and even under the pressures of a major exhibition experienced operators can relax and enjoy themselves.

The down side of this arrangement is cost and complexity. Although it is not necessary to incorporate full interlocking, detection circuits are required to ensure that the signal indications do correspond with the track settings. This is on top of the signals themselves and any panel indicators or illuminated track diagrams. There will inevitably be banks of relays, or racks of printed circuit boards, linked by a network of multi-core cables.

The alternative, telephonic communication via headsets and individual microphones, is reasonably effective. It has two inherent faults: the driver/operators are less free to move about, and verbal communication is notoriously imprecise. Apart from that, it just isn't railwaylike.

Telephonic communication can be useful at times, but is best provided by a handset that needs to be picked up before communication can take place. The important point is that on a well-organized system everyone knows what the next move should be. There is no need for discussion. The timetable tells everyone which train will be the next to run. If it is felt this information needs to be passed on, use a train describer.

The more common arrangement,

Early days at the Model Railway Club's 4 mm scale 'New Annington', before the advent of overhead wires and the new signalling; the old manual box is still there at the platform end. An 03 diesel mechanical shunter is moving a short rake of 16 ton steel-sided coal wagons into the yard, a sight that has disappeared from the model as well as the proto-type. One little-known feature of this layout is that the rolling stock has changed with the prototype. Indeed, the older DMUs were thankfully changed for Pacers and Sprinters, since the older stock was beginning to exhibit the same faults as BR's own sets, increasing unre-liability due to age.

where each operator has charge of a local panel, is much more simple. Here the operator is in the position of sig-nalman and has complete control over a clearly defined section of the layout. Signals are not necessary, since the operator is also the driver and knows which road has been set. Of course, he can still make a mistake, but once he is familiar with the controls it's a matter of self-discipline.

However, the need remains to communicate with the operators of adjacent sections. When the opera-tors are out of sight and earshot — as can happen on a garden layout, or on one where the line extends into two or more rooms — it is obvious that some form of remote communi-cation is needed, and this is usually done by a close copy of prototype

block signalling methods.

Block operation is also advisable when operators are in the same room. Agreed, they can speak with each other, but word of mouth communi-cation can be ambiguous. Block instru-ments on the other hand give a clear-cut indication at all times.

I have covered this aspect of oper-ation in *Model Railway Signalling* (published by Patrick Stephens Ltd in 1991), but it is of such importance that a recap is required. There are two sep-arate but linked elements, the block bells and the telegraph instruments. The former are very simple. Single-stroke bells are used to pass simple messages between operators. The lat-ter are a permanent reminder of the status of the section.

The protocol with block bells is sim-

Above *Waiting for the branch goods at Alan Wright's 'Cheviotdale'.*

Below *The diesel era on British Rail has seen several changes. This model scene depicts the first transition, when the green diesels and maroon coaches gave way to the blue-grey of the original TOPS period. The Hymek diesel is in green, the Mk 2A coaches are in blue-grey, as is the approaching three-car diesel, whilst the single parcels unit in the bay is in the original green with front feather.*

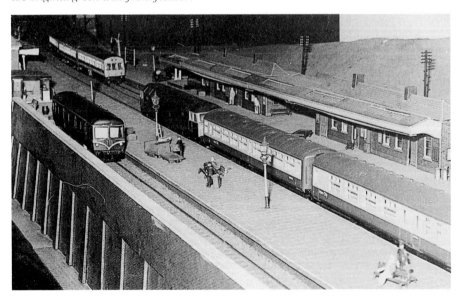

ple. The operator wishing to send a train gives a single ring, *Call attention.* The recipient acknowledges by repeating the call. The first operator then inquires *Is line clear for...* by means of a number of strokes, set out in Table 1. The recipient repeats the call when the line is clear and he is ready to receive the train. The first operator starts the train and sends *Train entering section* (two rings). On arrival the recipient sends *Train out of section* (two pause one ring).

Table 1 *Block bell train codes*

Is line clear for . . .train?	*Bell Code*
Express passenger	4
Ordinary passenger or mixed	3-1
Express parcels	1-3-1
Empty coaching stock	2-2-1
Fully fitted freight	4-1
Unfitted freight	1-4
Light engine	2-3

Note: The bell code refers to the beats and pauses: 1-3-1 is sent as one ring, pause, three rings, pause, one ring.

This is a simplification of the prototype system, and can be expanded to cover any additional information you feel is needed. Bell codes for branch trains and railcars might be worth adding should you feel the additional complications worthwhile. The basic messages above are adequate for most purposes. It could be worthwhile including the *Obstruction Danger* code, six consecutive beats, into the system, but one hardly needs to go into the ramifications of the prototype system.

Since block bells are fairly easy to arrange, they are very popular with serious operators. However there are two inherent snags. The first is that it can be difficult to distinguish between bell notes, particularly at an exhibition where the surrounding hubbub tends to make hearing difficult. The second is that there is no permanent reminder that train movements are taking place, which can be very awkward if, as is often the case, one or both operators cannot readily see the whole of the intervening stretch of track.

This is where block instruments are so useful. They are linked in pairs, one at each end, and provide three indications, *Line Blocked* (more recently *Normal*), *Line Clear* and *Train on Line.* The instrument normally shows *Line Blocked,* is changed to *Line Clear* when the operator receives the call on the bell, thus telling the other operator that the message has been received and understood. When the train enters the section, the instrument is turned to *Train on Line,* and only returned to *Line Blocked* when the *Train out of Section* message is received. The use of three rather than two indications reflects the basic principle of block working: the line is assumed to be blocked until a check has been made.

At one time prototype instruments were frequently used by model railway operators, which is very satisfying to the eye and the heart. Nowadays these magnificent examples of the instrument maker's craft are valued collector's items rather than unwanted relics of an outmoded operating system and cost as well as size suggests home-made replicas. I have, in *Model Railway Signalling,* described the construction of needle-type instruments, so I will deal with a different type, the light indicator.

Each instrument has three lamps, in light boxes, suitably masked and provided with a translucent overlay carrying the necessary legends. This is explained in Figure 37, which shows the basic parts of the instrument. Standard miniature Edison screw pattern lamps are used: the 12V types used for car dashboard panels are most suitable.

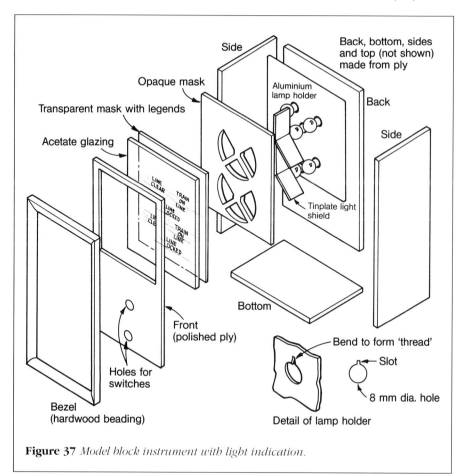

Figure 37 *Model block instrument with light indication.*

As the necessary lampholders are fairly costly and none too easy to obtain, I give details of a simple way of making a screw-in holder. You need a sheet of aluminium around 1mm thick of suitable size. Six holes 8mm in diameter are drilled to take the lamps, but before these are inserted a groove is cut in each hole and the sides of the groove twisted as shown in the sketch. This forms a very primitive but thoroughly effective thread into which the lamps can be screwed. This forms the common lead to the lamps; half a dozen small screws in a piece of 3mm ply form the other contacts.

The wiring diagram is shown in Figure 38, and requires little detailed

explanation, the lamps being controlled by a two pole three-way rotary switch. This allows the 12V lamps to be wired in series so that they can be used off the usual 16V ac auxiliary supply, with prolonged life, since replacement involves partially dismantling the instrument.

The instrument panel fits into a simple wooden box, or can be mounted alongside the control panel proper, according to taste and convenience. The push-button for the block bell is mounted beneath the rotary switch.

While the use of block bells and instruments might appear very fussy and complicated, I can vouch for the fact that it adds an extra dimension of

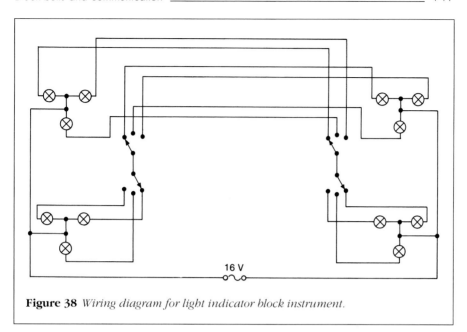

Figure 38 *Wiring diagram for light indicator block instrument.*

realism to model railway operation. It also meets the need to provide clear, uncluttered and, above all, unambigu- ous information to the layout opera- tors.

CHAPTER 14
Waybills and freight working

Until recent years, freight traffic formed a vital part of British railway operation. Indeed, those railways that were consistently profitable owed most of their revenue not to passenger traffic, but to a steady flow of coal trains over their metals. With the reduction in coal traffic and the switch from rail to road, modern freight working in Britain has shrunk to little more than block train working and container traffic, and diesel era models must reflect this change.

One could say that modern prototype practice has only followed the trend of many operating layouts, where although there were many different types of wagon to hand, goods trains were made up as blocks and shuttled from one end of the layout to the other. In extreme cases they would have a brake van at each end of the train to save time at the termini. Convenient though this might be from an operating standpoint, it deprives the operator of a fascinating feature of

Diesel era freight on the MRC's 'New Annington'. A class '58' diesel hauls an assorted train of long wheelbase air-braked four-wheeled stock on the main line. This corner of the layout has changed dramatically. The wood on the left and the buildings on the right have been swept away to make room for a motorway and new industrial units.

steam age operation. More to the point, it dispels the illusion of reality we are striving to present. Certainly, goods trains need to be shunted at stations, wagons left to be unloaded while loaded ones need to be taken away. On most layouts this is done, albeit in a fairly haphazard fashion.

Before we start to consider ways of giving this shuffling a greater resemblance of reality, it is worth giving a brief look at steam age freight operation. There were three types of train. The local or pick-up goods went around collecting and leaving wagons at the yards along its route, beginning and ending its run at a major concentration yard. There were trip workings, where complete trains were moved from one concentration yard to another, or between a concentration yard and a major industry, such as a coal mine, steel works, dock or large rail-served factory. These concerns frequently had an extensive rail network and a large collection of locomotives

which were fully occupied shunting the systems. Finally there were the marshalling or sorting yards, where the wagons collected from various parts of the system were shuffled into fresh trains for varying destinations. The last type of train was the through goods, which normally ran from the main marshalling yards to a concentration yard several hours' journey away.

Marshalling yards frequently incorporated a hump, a short, steep incline which gave the wagons a boost, whereupon they rolled down into the appropriate siding. Figure 39 shows an ideal marshalling yard in diagrammatic form. It will be seen that it is a very large item, well over five times as long as the longest train to be handled, which is why it is rarely modelled. It also needs a lot of wagons. The main snag is that the low inertia of model railway wagons makes it more difficult to get them to run freely down the tracks, while stopping them in the right place is also very tricky. It

Rail-connected industries have largely vanished in the diesel era, but during the steam age they provided an important source of traffic. Hatfield Maltings, on H.M. Pyrke's 'Berrow' branch, is a good example of an industry that once relied heavily on rail transport.

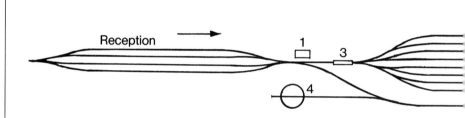

Figure 39 *Hump marshalling yard.*
Key:
1 Control tower; 2 Ground frame; 3 Hump; 4 Locomotive facilities; 5 Avoiding line for locomotives.

wasn't all that simple in full size to prevent heavy collisions and frequent derailments.

For model purposes, a simple flat concentration yard similar to that shown in Figure 40 is more convenient

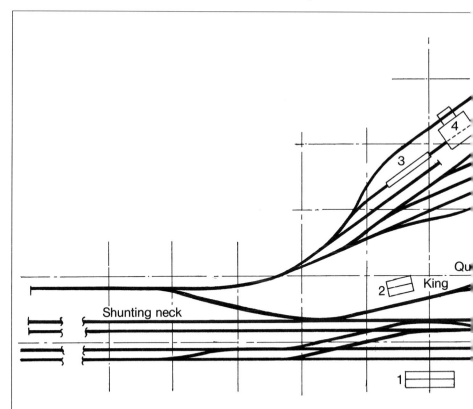

Figure 40 *Flat marshalling yard.*
Key:
1 Signal box; 2 Ground frame; 3 Ashpit; 4 Hopper coal plant; 5 Inspection pits; 6 Locomotive shed; 7 Turntable; 8 Wagon Repairs; 9 Brake vans.

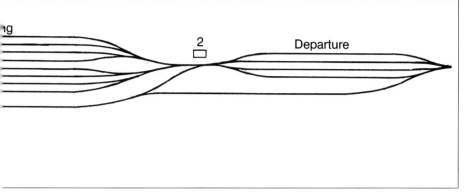

and less fraught with difficulties. A simple loop serves for arrival and departure, as well as a shunting spur, the parallel tracks are allocated to varying destinations. Wagons are put into the appropriate road. In such a yard there

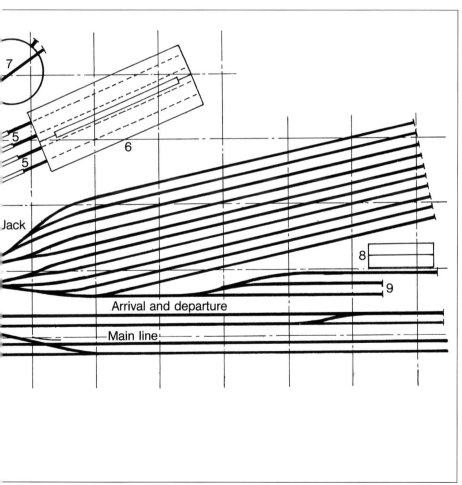

would be two more roads than standard destinations, since it was the practice to make a rough sort of the wagons to make up the completed train. Note the spur for brake vans and the siding beside the wagon repair works. The scheme also includes a locomotive depot, a frequent adjunct to main freight yards.

In order to get wagons to their proper destinations, each carried a waybill, which was securely held in a spring clip on the solebar so that the destination could be read from the lineside. There is little point in describing how this information was used on the prototype, since we have to diverge from full-size practice because even in the largest sized model, a scale-size waybill could only be read, with difficulty, using a powerful magnifying glass.

Waybills are probably superfluous on a single-station layout, since the operator will simply decide which wagons to transfer to and from the train. In the case of the popular terminus-fiddle yard layout, the position is obvious: every wagon on the train is assumed to be for that station. The only exception would be if there were a siding along the line without a run-round loop. In this instance, wagons for this siding would need to proceed to the terminus for reversal.

Where several goods yards are modelled, it is helpful to let the operator know which wagons are intended for him. One simple arrangement is to code each wagon with its destinations. This acknowledges the fact that when wagons are allocated to specific traffics, they tend to shuttle between a few

Britain's railways began with coal traffic which until the mid-1950s was an important feature of rail usage. Every station had its coal yard but surprisingly, except on the former North Eastern Railway, little use was made of coal drops. It was more common to shovel coal out of the wagons, often directly on to special scoop-fitted weighing machines in order to fill individual sacks with a full hundredweight. These coal drops at Peter Denny's 'Buckingham' are something of an exception but, as can be seen, they make an attractive model.

Before the advent of North Sea gas, every town of reasonable size possessed a gasworks, characterized by its distinctive gasholders. They were invariably rail connected, with a steady inward traffic of coal and outward loads of coke and coal tar.

destinations. As most model railways have only a handful of depots, it is possible to allocate each depot a distinctive colour, as in Table 2.

Table 2 *Colour codes for wagons*

Depot	Colour
Ayton	Red
Beeville	Yellow
Ceebury	Green
Deeford	Blue

Colour spots are placed unobtrusively on the wagon. Then, if the operator at Beeville receives a vehicle carrying a yellow spot, he knows he can remove it from the train and spot it in the appropriate siding. Each wagon has at least two spots, and so circulates around the layout in a fairly realistic fashion. There is a small limitation: the colours need to be distinctive, and so orange and purple — too easily mistaken for yellow and blue — are inadvisable, and brown

and black are likely to be too close to the wagon colour to be acceptable. In practice there are therefore just six colours available: white, grey, red, yellow, green and blue.

This system is somewhat inflexible, since the wagons will have a fixed circuit around the layout. Of course, a lot of regular traffic was worked by a small pool of vehicles which rarely strayed off a given route, so the system works smoothly with little or no appreciable loss of realism. It is certainly recommended as a starting system, but greater realism is possible if we can somehow provide waybills for the wagons.

While there is no practical way of fitting scale-sized waybills to individual wagons, it is possible to attach small coloured markers to serve the same purpose. With this system, the operator making up the train places the markers on the wagons, telling other operators along the line which vehicles to detach. Any unmarked wagon is deemed to be empty and can be detached by an operator needing that particular type of wagon, or returned to the fiddle yard as empty stock. As the markers are changed, one can extend the scheme to include bi-coloured markers, and both black and brown become acceptable. The only problem is how best to attach the markers, and the fact that they are of necessity fairly obtrusive and will be noticed by any visitors.

There is however no reason why the waybill has to be attached to the wagon: it can instead be placed in a wagon card. This is a piece of stiff card on which the essential details of the wagon are printed or typed. Clearly, each wagon needs to have a distinctive number, this will call for some work on ready-to-run vehicles which frequently are offered with just one running number. The card has a transparent plastic pocket attached into which a waybill is inserted. This pocket is cut from any convenient clear plastic sheet and held in place with self adhesive tape. Waybills are small enough to fit into the pocket without obscuring the wagon details and carry three bits of information, the load, the point of origin and the destination. Finally it is a good idea to have a train card, the same width as the wagon

card but longer, so that the train description can be read above the wagon cards. As this will get a lot of handling, it should be on thick card. Figure 41 shows the general arrangement and suggested dimensions, though these are obviously not critical.

In addition we need at each station at least six pockets, each large enough to hold several wagon cards, plus a train card and the waybills. Two are for the up and down trains respectively, one for the cards of wagons in the station, two (one inward, one outward) for the stack of waybills pertaining to that station and the last for spare train cards and a small supply of elastic bands. Figure 42 gives the general idea.

Operation begins by providing every station and fiddle yard on the layout with a stack of waybills denoting loads. How this is done must remain until the end: we'll deal with the straightforward part first. Each operator goes through his collection of waybills and starts to allocate the loads to the wagons in his possession by inserting the waybills into the appropriate wagon cards. Having done this, he can now assemble the train. Having done this, he takes the wagon cards, joggles them into a neat pile, attaches them to the train

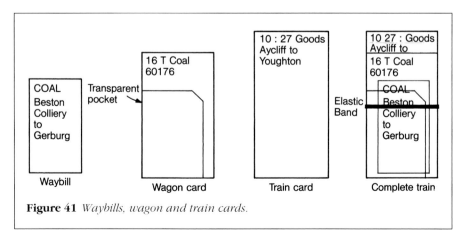

Figure 41 *Waybills, wagon and train cards.*

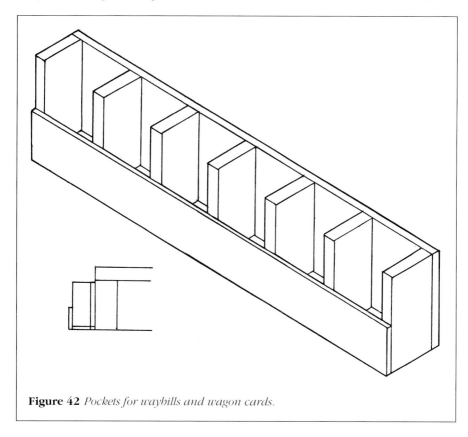

Figure 42 *Pockets for waybills and wagon cards.*

card with an elastic band and places the resulting train into the appropriate train pocket. When the train leaves, the train card and its collection of wagon cards and waybills is passed on to the next operator who looks through the collection to see which wagons he must detach, does so and then removes the appropriate cards from the pack and puts them into his wagon pocket. At the same time he transfers the wagon cards corresponding to the wagons he has attached to the train to the pack, puts an elastic band round the lot and passes the train and the train card to the next man down the line.

Two difficulties will quickly arise. The first is that train lengths are limited, not only by the length of loops and reception roads, but by the motive power available. Each locomotive should have an allocated load given in axles, which must not be exceeded. It will happen from time to time that there are more loaded wagons than can be taken away, in which case they have to wait for the next train, or the operator needs to have an extra train run solely to clear an overloaded station.

The second problem occurs when a load is offered for which a suitable wagon is not available. In this case the station operator has to find out where the wagon is and arrange to have it sent empty to his station. This is done by putting a despatch note, similar in size to a waybill but carrying the legend "Empty to Ceebury" in the wagon card and sending it on its way. This despatch note is also used to clear the

Another important rail-linked industry was the brickworks, with its characteristic kilns. Although the basic raw material, clay, was normally quarried close to the site, coal was needed in quantity, whilst the bricks were shipped out in open wagons. For obvious reasons the inward and outward traffic required different wagons; there is little demand for dirty bricks. This 7 mm scale model brick kiln is served by wagon turntables.

station yard of unloaded wagons which are surplus to requirements.

Waybills are produced to suit the collection of goods stock on the layout; clearly there is no purpose in making out documentation for loads which require a wagon that is not available. The specific loads, their point of origin and destinations will reflect the industries and communities on the layout, though with an offstage fiddle yard, one is not limited by the physical details of the model. There will be several waybills for each wagon, far more than would be needed for a normal operating session so that one can have a good deal of variety.

We now come to waybill allocation. In the most elementary method, they are put into a pack, shuffled and a predetermined number dealt out for each point of origin, the quantity depend-

ing on the throw of dice. It is worth mentioning that you are not limited to a six-sided die: several larger versions are obtainable from wargamers' suppliers. There should, of course, be a maximum set for each station.

Even when the waybills are randomly distributed, there is a possibility that they will come out in bunches. As they tend to get sorted into categories during use, this possibility becomes a probability and no amount of shuffling will cure this and a station can get some very unbalanced allocations. One way around this is to bias the distribution in favour of a preferred balance. In its simplest form this means setting a limit to the number of a specific type of loads for any one station. Should an additional waybill for this load be dealt, it is discarded and either replaced or the number of waybills is reduced.

Completely random selection ignores the fact that each station has its staple traffic. First on the list comes coal, which throughout most of the steam age was the keystone of British rail freight operation. So there will be a steady delivery of coal from one or more collieries, which will be conveniently offstage in most cases. An important point to remember with coal traffic is that the wagons were and indeed still are dedicated to the service, since they cannot be used for conveying other goods due to the dirty nature of the loads. This applies to other wagons used for minerals.

While coal was a steady traffic, it had its peaks and troughs, particularly if there was a manufacturing industry in the district whose requirements might vary. So we have a basic requirement for say five wagon loads of coal each day, with a variation of one either way. How do we determine this variation? We throw dice.

There will be other regular traffic, which can be predetermined in a similar fashion. For example, if there is a gasworks, there will be coal inward and coke and coal tar outward which again needs to be built into the schedule, though in this instance it is only likely to be subject to seasonal variations. However, a factory might not require the same sort of loads every working day. The more we fine tune the freight pattern at our stations, the less we leave to random chance.

Much of the preliminary work, in particular the planning of waybills, can be done anywhere at any time providing you have pencil and paper to hand to record your ideas. The system is capable of considerable refinement as your experience and knowledge of freight traffic operation grows: most users make detailed modifications to suit their own specific requirements. It is a good idea to prepare the loadings in advance by dealing the waybills and putting them into envelopes, which are then handed out to the various opera-

Although this 4 mm scale brickworks is, by model standards, quite large, it is actually a rather small affair. Full-size brickworks invariably had several kilns since the firing occupied several days and it was desirable to maintain a steady flow of bricks through the plant.

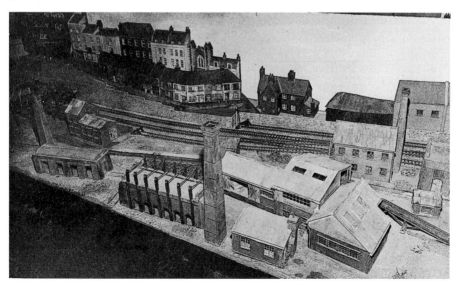

tors before running begins.

Freight operation can add immeasurably to the interest of steam age layout operation. What is more, there are many ways of setting about the business of deciding what loads are carried and where they are to go, those outlined above are only the main headings. They all are capable of considerable variation. If a system serves its main purpose, to ensure that goods wagons move about the system in a purposeful fashion, the exact details are unimportant. It is what you like that matters.

Which brings me to yet another method of allocating loads to wagons, the use of a home computer. At first sight it seems an ideal arrangement. For a start, the computer is not linked to the layout, it could even be in another place. In broad outline, several record files are set up; there will be a list of the wagons on the layout, a selection of appropriate loads,

together with point of origin and destination and a register of stations, together with their local industries. The program then makes a random selection from this information and produces a printout. Given suitable software, and programs do exist for this purpose, the process is automatic. Indeed, if you are really into computers, you will probably want to write your own program.

There is just one snag: it takes about as long to switch on the computer, load the program, make the necessary entries to set the system moving and then wait for the listing to be printed as it does to shuffle and deal a pack of waybills. With the computer system you then have either to match the waybills to the printout or, if the program prints out waybills, to cut them out of the fanfold paper. Computers are not necessarily quicker than paper and pencil methods.

Before we leave wagons, a word

A variety of wagon loads seen on Bob Harper's 'Maristow'. The wagon wheels in the right-hand wagon would have been an occasional load from a main works, needed to replace worn and even broken wagon wheels at this somewhat remote part of the system.

about loads. While a van looks the same whether loaded or empty, the same cannot be said of open wagons. Loads need to be provided for the ultimate realism, which brings us to the next point, the fact that loads have to be seen to have been delivered.

The answer is the removable load. Commercial loads which fit the manufacturer's wagons are available, though the ready-to-run concerns strangely enough do not generally provide this useful and attractive accessory. This is odd since at this end of the market the customer is less likely to be prepared to add his or her own loads.

The accepted arrangement for wagon loads is to provide a false top and fix the load to this. As shown in Figure 43, a wooden block is placed underneath so that the load is at the

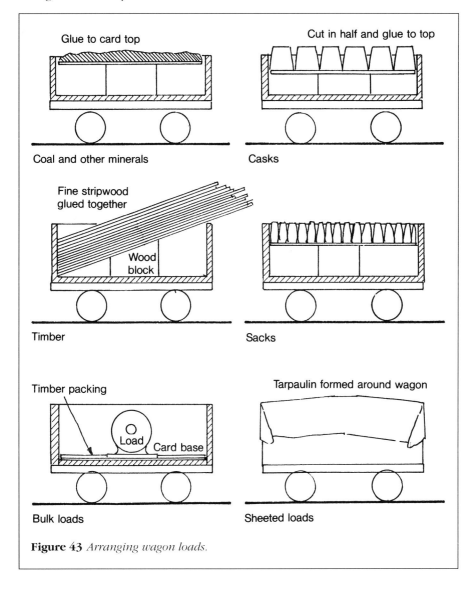

Figure 43 *Arranging wagon loads.*

right height and can also be easily removed.

The important point to consider now is when to exchange the loads. There are two schools of thought. One removes the load shortly after the wagon has arrived, regardless of the fact that an overscale hand is introduced into the model scene. The other method is to wait until the end of the model day and change loads in the timeless zone between this and the next operating session. Either method is equally valid.

It might be felt that at public exhibitions the introduction of the overscale hand into the model scene is doubly undesirable. This can be very much the case where great pains have been taken to arrange unobtrusive auto uncoupling. If we look at exhibition solely as a dramatic performance, this point of view has considerable validity. On the other hand, if we consider that an important function of model railway exhibitions is to instruct and inform, there is every reason to change wagon loads in full view of visitors. Someone is bound to say to himself, "So that's how it's done. I never knew it was so simple!", then go away and do it on his own model.

Coal and other minerals can be loaded into wagons from hoppers. This is a very popular exhibition gimmick and although it is normally associated with the toy end of the hobby, it is at its best when tackled by a serious modelmaker. Not only can one load wagons from hoppers, unloading, either by tipping the wagon or through bottom doors in hopper wagons, is also possible. The unloading mechanisms are the more intricate, but many minor difficulties are avoided if the wagons concerned are absolutely identical in size. This is most readily achieved by using a commercial vehicle.

CHAPTER 15
Special trains and unusual vehicles

Throughout this book I have dealt with the basic types of train and the general pattern of traffic that, with only minor local variations, is applicable to most British railways. In the initial stages of layout development this is sufficient to keep one very fully occupied, but after a while the simple pattern will begin to pall. This is the time to turn to what are generally termed specials. These fall into two separate categories, special vehicles for individual purposes and trains for specific traffic requirements.

The most common type of special train was so widespread it was not even regarded as a special. For the first half of this century, holiday-makers mainly travelled by train on a Saturday. This traffic peaked in the 1950s, and was particularly noticeable in the West Country, where everything was subordinated to the holiday rush. The popularity of the West Country branch as a prototype owes a lot to this traffic. Most of the preliminary field surveys were carried out during the annual holiday.

To meet the holiday rush, many trains were run in duplicate and even triplicate. Branches which at best enjoyed the luxury of a single through coach working received one or more complete trains of anything up to 12 coaches, if the platforms were long enough. As in the West of England the trains from London, the Midlands and the North did not arrive until well into the afternoon, the stock had to be stabled somewhere during the week in order to form the return working seven days later. Additional locomotives were needed, and frequently freight engines were pressed into service. In the final days, the BR standard '9F' 2-10-0 was very popular for this, because unlike all other freight engines, it could, if pressed, reach express speeds — providing you didn't mind repairing the track afterwards.

There were some interesting workings. The story of the Lyme Regis branch, and its three Adams 4-4-2 tanks, which worked one week on and two weeks off is well known. What is less well known is that the changeover took place on a Saturday so that both locomotives could haul the six-coach through train over the branch's stiff grades. Furthermore, in the 1950s, when the nearby Seaton branch had a through train, the returning Adams radial worked the branch set to Seaton since the regular 'M7' 0-4-4 had already gone down with the through rake of 10-plus coaches. Although few lines had quite so intricate a pattern, this weekly influx does provide a reason for introducing a deal of variety to an otherwise mundane traffic pattern.

While not in themselves special trains, slip coaches were a means of providing intermediate stations with a setting down connection from a non-stop train. This is very much a steam age feature which provided passengers with a fairly fast trip at the expense of loss of facilities, since the slip coach usually had no corridor connection to the rest of the train. The Great Western Railway was the most prolific user. It even went to the length of providing no less than three slip portions off its flagship service, the 'Cornish Riviera Express'. This made some sense, since the steady reduction in load roughly matched the steady increase in severity of the route's gradients. The last slip coaches ran on the Western Region.

Even on the prototype, dropping a slip coach and then having it coast to a standstill in the platform was by no means guaranteed. A pilot engine was always kept on standby to haul the coach in should it come to an ignominious halt outside the platform. On a model it is even more difficult to make a perfect slip and so the main interest in slip coaches lies in their use on branch line through services.

The most prestigious special is of course the Royal Train. While it might appear to be confined to main lines, it was the practice during Royal visits to

Devon to stable the train overnight on the Ashburton branch in a rather delightful stretch alongside the Dart. With this prototype justification, there is no reason why one cannot have the Royal Train put in an occasional appearance on any layout.

Apart from the Royal Saloons, there were other luxury coaches that were available for hire, if you had money to burn, while in more recent years there are the nostalgic rakes of restored vehicles, mostly, but not exclusively, Pullman cars. Another special coach that can be readily justified on any layout is the engineer's inspection saloon.

In between we have such things as mail trains, which might or might not have conveyed passengers. Of course rail-borne mail traffic has declined and the dramatic business of picking up and dropping pouches is a thing of the past, but for a steam age main line railway a mail train is a must. Whether you have mailbag pick-up is a matter of choice, since the need to make the mechanism operative means several parts have to be out of proportion.

Then there is the newspaper train.

Dean Goods 0-6-0 draws a goods train out of the yard on Ken Payne's 4 mm scale 'Castle Coombe'. The two leading wagons are bogie bolsters, used predominately for timber traffic but additionally employed for the carriage of rails.

A lot of timber was carried on twin four-wheeled bolster wagons, which ran as close-coupled pairs. Here we see two GW wagons in service on Bob Harper's 7 mm scale 'Maristow'.

Although the papers were carried in ordinary vans, the trains frequently had passenger coaches attached and provided an overnight service. The newspaper special from Waterloo to the West Country had the unique distinction for many years of not appearing in the public timetables, for all that it did convey anyone with a valid ticket who knew when it left, who didn't mind sleeping rough and arriving at the crack of dawn. Indeed, in its latter years one could use it to return to Devon on a cheap day ticket, despite the fact that it left in the early hours of the following day.

Another passenger-rated regular special is the milk train. Initially, milk travelled in churns, usually in slatted vans that kept everything nice and cool while on the run. In the 1930s the familiar glass-lined milk tank appeared and changed the traffic pattern. Whereas churns could be loaded at any raised platform, tanks had to be filled at special depots. It should be remem-bered that the systems are mutually exclusive; you can't have churns and tank wagons at one and the same time.

Oil and petrol were also carried in tank wagons. Although we associate these with petrol and the growth of road traffic, kerosene was used for illumination at the dawn of the railway age. Initially, it was carried in casks in open wagons. The familiar tank wagon did not make an appearance until the latter years of the nineteenth century. As petrol traffic grew, depots were set up to handle this at major centres. These comprised a siding with stand-pipe for unloading, underground storage tanks and, most noticeable of all, a special building inside a secure fence with a fire break all round in case of accident. It is illegal as well as dangerous to decant highly flammable liquids directly into road tankers or, worse still, individual cans.

During much of the nineteenth century and the early part of the twenti-eth century, the theatre was the

During the steam age, cattle traffic was very important and frequently special trains were run in connection with cattle markets. This train, headed by a GWR 0-6-0 pannier tank, contains a variety of cattle wagon types sharing the same characteristics: large, full-height twin-centre doors and open upper sides with lower slits for drainage. The white marking is limewash, once liberally applied at the end of each trip but discontinued just before the end of rail-borne cattle traffic when it was belatedly discovered that it affected the beasts' hoofs.

principal form of entertainment. It was divided into three strands, the local repertory company, the music hall, and the travelling companies. Music hall artistes could normally get all their personal props and costumes into a couple of large hampers, which went with them by train. As they travelled on Sundays and so experienced a very basic service punctuated by delays caused by track repairs, it is understandable that they took a jaundiced view of the system. Hence the number of references to changing trains at Crewe and the long waits involved. The touring companies not only travelled as a group, they also needed to take the various flats that formed the scenery, as well as bulky items of stage furniture. In due course the larger railway companies produced special-purpose long vans with end doors for this traffic. Most of them outlived the traffic.

On occasions a farmer decided to move from one end of the country to the other, taking with him his livestock and implements. This involved a special train that had a single coach for the family and any employees who were moving as well, vans for their household goods, cattle trucks for the livestock, together with vans and implement wagons for the farm machinery.

One type of special train is virtually confined to the USA, the circus train. In Britain and to a large extent in Europe, circuses have always preferred the road. This is because distances between towns large enough to support a circus performance are short enough to make even a horse-drawn wagon tolerable. As soon as effective traction engines became available, circuses adopted them. Once electricity generation was developed, the traction engine also provided power and light in a more friendly, if more hazardous, fashion than today's mobile generators.

The traction engine was powerful but slow, so when it was necessary to move it any considerable distance it was put on the rail. A special wagon, the four-wheeled implement wagon, was designed for this and other large road vehicles, and remained in production right into the post-war period.

This was not by any means the first time road vehicles went by rail. The carriage wagon, attached to the rear of a train, goes back to the origins of passenger traffic. The upper classes initially made considerable use of this service, leading to the rapid decline of posting inns. Initially the owners rode in their own carriages, but this did not last long, since first-class compartments were positively luxurious and even a good second gave better seating than many private coaches. By the middle of the nineteenth century this traffic had virtually died out.

There was a sudden revival around the turn of the century when the motor car came into being. The early models were prone to breaking down after a relatively short distance, and so it was quite common for an Edwardian motorist to load his car into a four-wheeled van and have it taken to the area he wished to tour. These vans were also used to transport cars from the factories to the selling points, and this type of vehicle survived until quite recently as the CCT (covered carriage truck). Before the motorway network existed, many holiday-makers found it less stressful and certainly quicker to put their cars on a car-carrier train. At the outset, CCTs were the normal vehicle used, but now cars are conveyed in bogie GUVs (general utility vans). The modern car transporter is just the latest in a long line, and may well proliferate with the opening of the Channel Tunnel.

Until quite recently there was an enormous variety of special-purpose vehicles for specific traffics. Probably the most bizarre were the corpse vans.

A rare four-wheeled GWR Siphon on Frank Colson's 4 mm scale 'Modbury'. Its short length and simple wheelbase makes it very suitable for layouts with sharp curves in limited spaces.

Above *The LMS used many short six-wheeled passenger rated vans, a practice inherited from the Midland Railway. This is an example of a Derby-built van in 7 mm scale on Norman Eagles' 'Sherwood' section.*

Below *LMS six-wheel and bogie passenger vans on H.M. Pyrke's 'Berrow' branch.*

There were very few of these since apart from the LSWR, which did the job in style with its service from Waterloo (Necropolis platform) to Brookwood, railways discouraged this type of traffic. The narrow gauge Festiniog had one, which says a lot about the working practices in the quarries. So did the North British, who also had a prison van.

This brings us neatly to the bullion van, normally a very plain steel-sided vault on wheels. The last such vehicles, built by British Rail just after the Great Train Robbery, had a compartment at one end for the security guards. For obvious reasons they did not have corridor connections, and were converted from Mk I stock.

Many special freight vehicles are closely linked to specific industries. In particular, the steel industry had a range of wagons for conveying molten or merely hot metal around the plant, only venturing on to the main lines on rare occasions and then never when in use. The modern nuclear flask wagons are also 'hot' and are a frequent load over specific routes, always in the early hours to avoid the denser traffic and the attention of the public at large. There has never been any great secret about them, despite the occasional flurry of outrage in local papers when someone discovers that they have been running through the district for years without incident.

Until comparatively recently the railways had on hand a range of heavy-duty wagons that could be used for a wide variety of loads. The most versatile were the heavy bogies that could take a range of girders to transport almost anything, ranging from transformers on the one hand to naval guns on the other. Except as part of through

The Southern Railway built a large number of these four-wheeled General Utility vans for use with passenger trains. They remained in service well into the diesel era and from the outset could often be seen well away from their parent railway. They were extremely useful and apt to be borrowed by other operators.

GWR Crocodile H well wagon carrying a small marine pattern boiler load. This commercial model is notable for the lack of the numerous chains and timber packing that would be needed to secure the boiler in transit.

traffic, such vehicles are difficult to justify on a model railway, while their size tends to make them an over-prominent feature in the train. The more common well wagon, which was designed for bulky loads, is easier to justify, except on a feeder branch. There were a few wagons designed for specialized loads. The propeller truck, which could transport medium-sized ship's propellers, is extremely difficult to justify. The glass wagon, which held sheets of plate glass vertically between a light girder frame, is the sort of wagon that can find a place on most steam age layouts, since every community has its shops, and shops have large windows that, from time to time, get broken. In the steam age, rail transport was the most practical way of taking large sheets of glass any appreciable distance.

The problem with all special wagons is providing a sound reason for their appearance on the layout. Of course, one can add a suitable rail-connected industry, but leaving aside any question of finding the space, there is also the question of probability. A

community can only support so many diverse industries. However, it is as well to remember that whereas on the prototype the industries preceded the wagons, on most model railways the wagons come first and the industry is added to justify the wagon.

There is one special wagon that needs little excuse, one that until fairly recently was quite common. It is the gas tank wagon, built to carry gas under pressure from the central plants to outlying stations, where it was used to fill the cylinders under the coaches. Although electric lighting came into general use over 80 years ago, gas remained in use until the 1950s. It was particularly so on short branches, where the daily mileage was barely sufficient to recharge the batteries on electrically lit stock. A gas-lit vehicle was easy to recharge, and before the full development of mains electricity to the more remote areas of Britain the only practical solution. It has yet to appear as a ready-to-run model, but then very few special-purpose wagons are so available, though many are produced as kits.

CHAPTER 16
Keeping them working

It is very easy to discuss the operation of model railways at length without considering what is by any standards the most important factor of all, the reliability of the layout. One must also consider the operation of Murphy's Law, which in its general case states unequivocally that if a thing can go wrong, it will go wrong.

Model railways provide an almost infinite number of demonstrations of Murphy's Law. This is a consequence of one of its important clauses that the more devices you connect in series,

the more likely you are to reach the point where one will fail every time. If you think 90 per cent reliability is good, think again. It actually means that there is a distinct probability it will go wrong once every 10 times you use it. Put 10 such devices together and *wham*, it is unreliable. Luckily most model railway equipment is 99.999 per cent reliable, but that odd 0.001 per cent can create havoc. There is also the good old factor, operator error to consider. We all make mistakes.

One of the most baffling faults on

This 4 mm scale Class '110' DMU by Hornby makes a convenient local train for a post-1950 layout with an emphasis on intensive operation. Capable of being driven from either end, the set does not require elaborate facilities at each end of the run and is perfectly happy with a simple bay road, long enough to allow it to stand within platform limits.

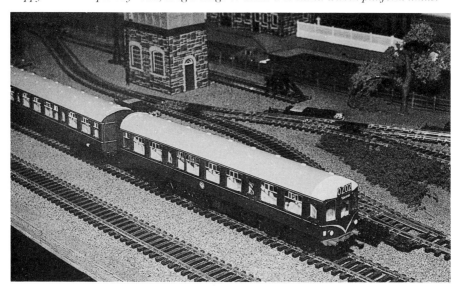

A brief reminder of the former staple traffic of British railways, coal in the form of a train of North Eastern Railway hoppers hauled by a Stockton & Darlington 0-6-0 long-boilered coal hauler.

any model railway (or other mains-powered equipment come to that) occurs when someone has removed the mains plug from its socket and failed to replace it. Even worse is the case where the plug is in place but the switch is turned off. Most annoying of all is when the 3A fuse in the plug top decides to expire for no obvious reason. This is why most advanced workers put a 'power on' indicator somewhere on the main panel. No light means no power, so check back to the plug that is usually in a near inaccessible location.

Another baffling fault occurs when the road is not correctly set. Usually this means the train ends up in the wrong place, but occasionally it simply doesn't move. Even the most experienced of operators can fall into this trap and spend time looking for short circuits, checking if the loco is OK and generally running through a series of tedious and, in the event, unnecessary checks before discovering what ought to be obvious, but isn't.

Let's assume that the road is set up, all appropriate section switches are on, power is supplied to the controller, but still nothing happens. What then? The first thing to check is whether there is an overload or not, because if so you might be in real trouble. Ninety-nine times out of a hundred the overload indicates a short circuit caused by something lying across the track, the hundredth is caused by a jammed locomotive. In this instance, keeping power on the circuit will quickly cook the armature windings. If you wait for the loco to send up distress signals — a thin sliver of smoke and a nasty smell — it will be too late, so assume the worst and lift the loco off the track. If this clears the fault, continue the lifting until the locomotive is on the workbench for overhaul.

Short circuits on the track are less serious but much more trouble, since they can be anywhere. If the layout is properly sectioned, you can energize each section in turn until you find the offending one. Occasionally you may find that each section is clear, so you now switch on adjacent sections until you find which pair are interacting. This tells you that it's probably a fault in the wiring, but it can happen when a coach or wagon with a metal chassis is standing over a section break where power is opposed.

Once you've located the offending section, reverse each point in turn. This can help to narrow the area of search. Pay particular attention to pointwork, since this is where opposing polarities come close together and a small pin or length of wire in the wrong place can give you trouble out of all proportion to its size. Bits of metal lying across the track are fairly obvious. Except, of course, on hidden tracks where you can't see anything; the only redeeming quality is that things are less likely to fall on to a covered section.

Always remember that even on a permanent layout, parts of the base-board can move as the wood expands and contracts with variations of temperature and humidity. Rails also expand and contract with temperature changes. These two factors make it all too easy for the rails on either side of a section break to come together with dire consequences. This is unlikely to happen when the break has been made with an insulating rail joiner, since these normally have a plastic fin in the centre for the express purpose of avoiding this problem. However, when a break is made by cutting through the rail in situ, as is inevitable if one adds an extra section after the track is laid, the possibility of closure is present. The best solution is to fill the gap with a little quick-setting epoxy resin, which is an extremely effective insulator. Needless to say, the surplus resin needs to be removed after it has hardened, and under no circumstances should you run trains over the track until this has happened; allow 24 hours to be on the safe side.

LNWR 'Precursor' class 4-4-0 leaving the up slow platforms on Bill Oakes' 'Berkhamstead' model.

It is not a good idea to have a section break coincide with a baseboard joint on a sectional layout. Any movement of the joint can cause the rails to come into contact and one must always expect some shift in the relative position of sectional baseboards. Apart from movement of the framing timber, it is inevitable that someone will lean against the baseboards at some time.

Short circuits can occur in the wiring. Mostly this is down to faulty wiring technique, allowing too much bare wire at critical points. The compact computer pattern multi-way plugs and sockets are particularly prone to this problem, so it is essential that all joints should be shrouded with a short (approximately 10 mm) length of insulating sleeving. The use of multi-strand flexible wire is another source of trouble, since it is all too easy for a stray strand to make contact across a gap. One can also add to the list the use of too much solder, with the result that the large blob goes where it shouldn't, but as this fault is present at the outset, it ought to be eliminated before running begins.

We have already mentioned the possibility of rolling stock bridging a section gap, and it is also necessary to point out that a derailed wagon or coach can cause trouble, as can a long coupling link that just happens to touch a rail. With modern construction techniques, particularly the use of plastics and, more important still, the fact that most metal wheels are fully insulated so that the axle is not connected to either rail, this problem does not arise until coach lighting is fitted, with pick-ups on the wheels. There are a few cases where coach pick-up has been arranged by having the wheels on one side connected to the axles. If for any reason one wheel set gets reversed, you have trouble.

These are the most common causes of short circuits, but there are others. There was a case where a track pin touched a screw holding an inter-baseboard contact, leading to a mysterious fault that took over a week to track down. There are a number of other similar improbable ways of cross-connecting circuits you fondly believe are completely separate. Unfortunately, because of their unpredictable nature they are extremely difficult to locate. Often the only possible solution is to start cutting the wiring away until the rogue circuit is eliminated, then replacing everything in a more methodical fashion.

The apparent absence of current in the rails is rather less fraught with difficulty. It is basically a matter of working steadily from one end or the other, checking with a meter or a simple light probe until you track down the point of break.

On a sectional layout, where there must be inter-baseboard and control panel–baseboard links, check these first. Push in all plugs, check contacts between baseboard units. Suspect the condition of jumper cables. It is very easy for the wires to fracture near the ends where movement is greatest. Needless to say, all wiring that is subject to movement must be made with flexible multi-strand wire. Employing single-core wire for this purpose is asking for trouble.

Another cause of trouble is the dry joint, a soldered connection made with insufficient heat. The annoying thing about this fault is that although most dry joints show up at once, some take a couple of years to crystallize and convert what was once a minimal resistance connection into a near perfect insulator at low voltages. Another difficulty arises when an old, tarnished tag on a switch or tag strip was only partially cleaned when the joint was made. It is always a good idea to tin all tags before soldering the wires to them.

A common method of getting around a disconnection is to solder a fresh length of wire around the break. This can be carried too far, as an old friend once remarked: 'Half these wires are doing nothing, I could take them out if only I knew which half they were.' Long before you get to this point you should seriously consider a comprehensive rewiring programme since you have clear-cut evidence of a very serious state of affairs.

Although we have given short circuits and disconnections a lot of attention, the commonest cause of poor running is gunge. This is not dirt, it is a fiendish concoction with a strong oil base. While many people suggest it is the result of over-enthusiastic oiling, another cause is air pollution, in particular that from car exhausts. Mixed with dust, this film forms everywhere.

It is a relatively simple if tedious business to burnish the tracks before operation, using either a track-cleaning rubber, a fibreglass-cleaning stick or, in extreme cases, fine abrasive paper. There is currently a very effective HO gauge track cleaning vehicle made by Roco that has an abrasive pad fitted between the wheels. It is of course equally effective in OO gauge and has been adapted to HOm (12 mm) gauge as well.

Track cleaning wagons involving solvents do not appear to be very effective. Indeed although various sprays and solvents have been tried, most seem to end up leaving an even more tenacious film on the railhead. Most solvents give off fumes that are highly toxic in any appreciable concentration and are therefore not a good idea.

Track cleaning is a fairly obvious course, but wheels are another matter. While regular running helps, gunge does tend to build up during a running session. All too often only the locomotive wheels involved in pickup are cleaned and the rest of the stock ignored. Often the build-up of gunge around the root of the flange is clearly visible to the naked eye. Not only is this deposit putting gunge back

LNER 'K3' 2-6-0 No 1345 waits in the sidings outside Geoff Bigmore's 'Bigston' with a recently arrived freight train backed up behind.

A train of BR Mk 1 coaches in Southern green arrives at H.M. Pyrke's 'Berrow' behind an 'LMS '4F' 0-6-0.

on to the rails, it has also been known to reach the point where the running is seriously affected because the flange depth has been reduced. Plastic wheels are particularly prone to gunge build-up, which is the main reason why many people claim that metal wheels have better running qualities. Gunge is best removed from wheel treads with the business end of a small screw-driver (Figure 44), or a fine fibreglass brush.

As I said earlier, oil is an important constituent of gunge. One source of this is over-generous oiling of loco-motives and the use of the wrong oil. So let's begin by dealing with the biggest cause of trouble, 3-in-1 oil. This mixture contains a particularly gooey constituent that not only adheres to track and wheels, but is also apt to play havoc with plastics as well. What-ever its virtues may be elsewhere, as far as we are concerned it has none.

There are many lubricants formulated for our type of work. For some years I have been using Daywat; I have also used Singer sewing-machine oil. Watchmakers have a suitable oil, but with the switch to quartz drive in clocks and watches both watchmakers and watch oil are hard to find.

Whatever oil you use, it needs to be applied sparingly. Although there is from time to time a burst of enthusi-

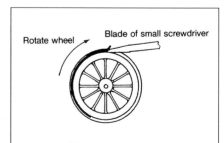

Figure 44 *Removing gunge from wheel tyres.*

asm for hypodermic syringes, I remain faithful to a much older method, a length of stiff wire as shown in Figure 45. This has many merits. It is cheap, easily replaced, it will get into the narrowest of gaps and deliver a tiny drop of lubricant just where you want it *and nowhere else*. All you need do is dip it into the bottle and apply the small drop to the bearing. Should you want to apply more than just a tiny drop, a very small loop of about 0.5 mm diameter at the end of the wire will do the trick. Gears are best lubricated by a minimal smear of light grease. Vaseline or similar petroleum jelly is fine for the job.

Avoid getting any oil on to traction tyres. This plays havoc with the tyres, softening the synthetic rubber and depositing a particularly nasty form of gunge on the track. These tyres do need replacing from time to time, but on steam-outline locomotives this is easier said than done. Many enthusiasts go to the trouble of replacing the wheel sets, which is sometimes easier

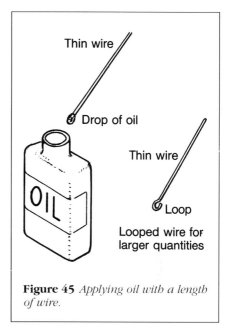

Figure 45 *Applying oil with a length of wire.*

than replacing the tyres. A lot depends on whether the layout's grades have been laid out to take advantage of the traction tyres, since if one relies on the extra grip then clearly one has to live

LMS local train, headed by an ex-Midland 0-6-0T, forerunner of the standard LMS design, comprising a selection of different non-corridor compartment vehicles. A cattle wagon waits at the nearby cattle loading dock.

with the inherent problems of the tyres. It is a matter of compromise and opinion which course is best.

All rolling stock needs periodic maintenance. On a large layout with an extensive collection of locomotives, coaches and wagons, some form of record-keeping is really needed so that everything gets a regular check rather than waiting until trouble rears its ugly head. For smaller layouts there are two well-tried methods. The most obvious is to institute regular maintenance sessions, when everything is checked over. The other is to have a surplus of stock, so that there is always a spare locomotive, coach or wagon to replace those that show the slightest sign of trouble. These defective items are set aside for attention at a later date.

All sensible maintenance plans involve specific sessions of overhaul and repair. This allows one to set out the workbench for the task, with all the necessary equipment laid out to hand. In particular, you need a stock cradle. Special foam plastic blocks are made for this purpose, and while costing more than the home-made alternative — a wooden trough lined with foam plastic offcuts — they are much more convenient to use, having no hard edges and being far less likely to skid off the edge of the working surface.

Most locomotives are sold with an instruction sheet detailing the procedures to be followed. Most instruction sheets are lost and even when one puts them away in a safe place it usually works out that by the time you need them you've forgotten where it is. The methodical few file the sheets. The best way I know is to slip them into transparent A4 pockets and put these into a labelled ring binder. On a permanent layout, this binder would stand on a small shelf under the layout alongside the wiring book.

Digressing slightly, I find these pock-ets absolutely invaluable for holding important papers, since they keep the documents safely in a place they can readily be seen and there is little or no risk of their being thrown away with the rubbish. They cost (1993) about 11p apiece if bought in small quantities, but if you keep your eyes about you, you can get them much cheaper at sale times, or by buying in bulk.

Back to locomotive maintenance. Hopefully you have the instruction sheet, which will tell you how to take the darned thing apart, but failing that you will have to apply your mind to the subject. There are two methods used to attach the locomotive body to the chassis, screws and clips. The screws can be seen by inverting the model. It is often necessary to remove the bogie or pony truck from a steam locomotive to reach the fixing screw. The number of screws used varies not merely with the manufacturer, but also with the locomotive. In practice only one fixing screw at the front and a single tenon fixing at the back is needed to hold a steam locomotive chassis in place. Unfortunately many manufacturers who adopt this simple scheme also use the fixing screw to secure the cylinder block as well, which makes reassembly a shade fraught.

Many bodies on ready-to-run diesel and electric locomotives simply clip over the underframe carrying the power bogies. Removing these bodies involves springing the sides apart which, if you don't know the trick, can be a shade fraught. A few small wedges (in practice the ubiquitous matchstick) are usually needed to keep the sides apart as you methodically release all the catches. I wish they wouldn't use this method. A screw fore and aft is much more reliable. However, another trick is to put a screw through the top and then hide it under a removable roof fixture. A similar problem can arise when a designer decides to secure a steam locomotive body to the chassis with a blackened screw through the chimney. This is OK if you know which fixture to remove, or realize that the screw is there in the first place. Otherwise you can spend a long time wondering why the body refuses to budge.

You will now have several loose parts, most of which are of no immediate interest. It is essential to put these into a container and not leave them lying about the workbench where they will get lost.

Once the works are out of the body, you can set about maintenance. The first thing to do is to look for any fluff or hairs that have got inside. These need to be removed with tweezers, or occasionally you may need to winkle the more obstinate ones out with a pin. Excess muck can be wiped away with cotton buds and then fresh oil applied sparingly to all bearings. It is worth repeating that only a *very* small quantity of a light oil sold for the purpose by a reputable dealer should be applied directly to the bearings and other moving parts *and nowhere else*. Figures 46 and 47 indicate the main points to observe when maintaining a locomotive chassis.

While the works are out of the body, run your eye over the internal electrics. These are normally very

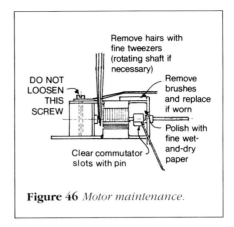

Figure 46 *Motor maintenance.*

straightforward and rarely give trouble. When they do you know all about it since the locomotive just refuses to function. Pick-ups are generally the most troublesome part of the locomotive, and the tension on any wheel-back wipers is fairly critical. Increasingly manufacturers are adopting more sophisticated methods which avoid wheel pick-ups, though this is largely confined to diesel and electric outline models. Whatever method of pick-up is used, it fails if the wheel treads are dirty. Regular wheel-cleaning is advisable on all stock, and on locomotives it is essential.

It is customary to give each locomotive chassis a power test before reassembly. This generally involves a good deal of juggling and so it is a

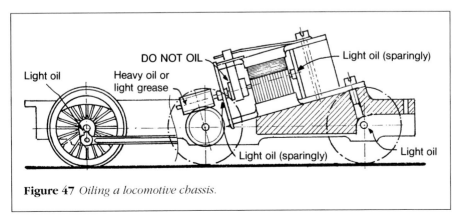

Figure 47 *Oiling a locomotive chassis.*

good idea not only to have a power supply on the bench, but to have the leads terminate in crocodile clips so you can attach them to a suitable part of the mechanism. A locomotive test bed, with rollers on which the driving wheels can sit, is an extremely useful adjunct to the workbench.

Coaches and wagons can usually be cleaned and oiled without any need to dismantle any parts. On the other hand, automatic couplings frequently need adjustment. This implies a special jig, consisting of a length of track fitted to a board with a spare coupling fixed at the correct height at one end so that the alignment of couplings may be checked.

We come now to the big bugbear of all operators, derailing. There are three main causes, operator error, track misalignment and incorrect wheel setting. Operator error is mainly a matter of running at excessive speeds or of failing to set the route correctly and its cure is a matter of self-discipline. Track misalignment and wheel faults are more difficult to put right.

The biggest problem is deciding what is actually at fault. The simple rule of thumb is that if derailments occur at a particular spot, the track is at fault, whereas if they occur with specific vehicles then the trouble lies here. This is true for gross faults, but usually it is a combination of a slightly defective vehicle and a slightly dodgy bit of track.

It goes without saying that you should check track gauge, flange clearances and wheel settings with care. Putting the faults right is another thing

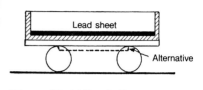

Figure 48 *Adding ballast to an open wagon.*

altogether. Dodgy track and points are best replaced, because any attempt to adjust in situ usually only makes matters worse. Troublesome wheels can be replaced. Re-setting a misaligned wheel set is a fairly skilled operation. Even if you're up to the task, it is probably easier to replace the wheels and put the vehicle back into service. The wheels can be then dealt with in a batch.

One cause of derailment is lack of weight. If a vehicle persistently dances off the track, try the effect of a ballast weight before anything else. Often a piece of lead sheet (Figure 48) will do the trick; once the right-size piece is determined, it can be held in place with a dab of glue.

Point motors, if properly fitted and correctly operated, rarely give trouble. However, the common double solenoid motor is a crude device that can be easily overloaded. It is advisable to operate this type of motor through a capacitor discharge unit. This not only sends a powerful surge through the coil and ensures a good snap action, it also prevents the coil overheating should the flash switch stick.

Index